on
SCAMMELL

Published by
KELSEY PUBLISHING LTD

Printed in Singapore by Stamford Press PTE Ltd
On behalf of
Kelsey Publishing Ltd,
Cudham Tithe Barn,
Cudham,
Kent, TN16 3AG
Telephone: 01959 541444. Fax: 01959 541400

ISBN 1 873098 59 6

Acknowledgements
Barnaby Newton, Mike Jeffries, Nick Baldwin, Peter Davies, Bill Robins,
Alec Kermotschuk, Graham Edge, Brian Timms, David Reed, Nick Larkin, Pat Ware
and *Classic Military Vehicle*.

Front cover
*Former Blue Circle 1981 Scammell Routeman, superbly
restored by Dave Pearson (photo: Glyn Barney).*

INTRODUCTION

Scammell. Even the word has a solid, dependable and individual ring to it – and the same goes for the products of Watford-based Scammell Lorries Ltd., right from its first vehicle in 1922, a six-wheel artic.

The company's history indirectly goes back to 1837 however, with the formation of coachbuilders – later steam wagon repairers – G Scammell and Nephew Ltd., based at Spitalfields, London. Scammell's reputation grew through the 1920s with the highly successful 6x4 and 6x6 Pioneers and then in 1929 came a masterpiece, the Scammell 100 tonner, with massive trailer and steerable rear bogie. Only two were built, both leaving the factory with the company's own seven-litre four-cylinder engine – and needless to say, the vehicles weren't marketed for their performance.

Until the early 1930s all vehicles were chain drive operated, but this period would see many changes, including the fitting of Gardner diesel engines and a highly successful gamble to focus away from heavyweight trucks and produce the legendary Mechanical Horse. Superb vehicles such as the Rigid Eight followed, which would remain in production for more than 20 years, and the company also became Britain's biggest trailer manufacturer. World War Two saw many Scammells in military service, and postwar heavy tractor units such as the Explorer, Mountaineer and Constructor also did well.

In 1955 Scammell was taken over by Leyland, but its identity, factory and products remained. In 1958 came the fibreglass-cabbed Routeman, replaced four years later by a Routeman II, with cab designed by Giovani Michelotti, who normally devoted his attentions to sports cars. This would be replaced by the Leyland Constructor in 1980 – a vehicle developed by Scammell as part of its heavy vehicles range.

Sadly, though, Scammell was a victim of the DAF/Leyland 'merger,' and the Watford plant closed in 1988. Inspect a Scammell today though, and even the most anti-lorry campaigner would marvel at the sheer quality and indestructibility of a finely – if heavily-engineered – product.

This book aims, through the reprinting of articles from *Classic and Vintage Commercials*, along with some from our sister publication *Classic Military Vehicle*, to convey the true essence of Scammell. Not only have we selected articles on everything from Mechanical Horses to the mighty LA, but we have looked at the people who have driven and operated Scammells. We also take the story forward to recent times, for not only are some Scammells still earning their keep, but others are being returned to their glory by dedicated restorers.

Thanks to them we can see classic Scammells where they ought to be – out on the road!

Nick Larkin,
Editor,
Classic and Vintage Commercials.

CONTENTS

OUR FLING WITH SCAMMELL HIGHWAYMAN DLK 380C

Barnaby Newton tells the story of the Scammell that his family fleetingly owned

All photographs by Barnaby Newton

For a road steam enthusiast like myself internal combustion commercial vehicles meant the end of the road for our beloved steam vehicles, like Foden, Sentinel, Thornycroft, Yorkshire and so on.

on. Still, as Scammell progressed into becoming vehicle manufacturers as Scammell and Nephew then at Spitalfields, they were service agents for Foden and Sentinel steam vehicles. So perhaps that's why steam people have a great passion for Scammell vehicles. For me another

take our fleet of engines about was quite a sensible one and highly desirable, so the search was on.

After many phone calls and letter writing we finally tracked one down close to home near Newbury in Berkshire; we went to view this tractor unit straight away. The Scammell was tucked away in a shed and was rather dusty; still it was what we wanted. The Scammell was a Highwayman registration DLK 380C, built in 1965, with a 680 Leyland engine and had been part of the large Shell-Mex fleet. It still had the skirt behind the engine and exhaust pipe fitted to keep the risk of sparks down to a minimum. Anyhow, my father, John Newton, decided it was what we wanted. Our good friend Gordon Hedges from Newbury, who at the time ran a coach company, agreed to take the Scammell out for a road test. So we duly started the vehicle up and Gordon gave the vehicle a good road test and a visual check over at the local coach station over the pit where we could see things more clearly. Gordon has an HGV licence whereas we don't, so he became extra useful! His conclusion on the 1965 Scammell was that it was in good condition mechanically, even having a high speed rear axle fitted; we nearly reached 60 mph on the way to the coach station.

It was in November 7 1979 that we purchased the Highwayman for £675 and brought it back to Hungerford where the rebuilding of the bodywork was to began. We started to strip the panel work off, also the window mechanisms as they didn't work very well. The cab needed patching up because it is glassfibre; we repaired this and added Isopon filler where required and much filling and rubbing took place in a short space of time. It was cleaned off and hand-primered all over, followed with two coats of undercoat red, which we heavily rubbed down. We enlisted the help of Pat Munday, former paint sprayer foreman at Lambourn Coach Works and he readily agreed to spray the unit for us. We decided to go for the same colour as our 5hp Burrell Road Locomotive *John of Grant*, which is maroon. The Scammell bodywork was sprayed maroon and the undercarriage, so to speak, was painted bright red. We masked the whole job up around the mirrors, windsrceens and so on. Peter Legg, who is the fourth generation of the family who are signwriters, came down from Newbury to carry out the job. We decided to line out the Scammell in the same style as the Burrell, the colours being black, red and yellow. Then we decided to name the Scammell after father's nickname, *The*

Just after Gordon Hedges had brought the vehicle back from checking it out in late 1979.

However, some of these companies lasted into the I/C era and Foden do still exist today. When thinking of a make of lorry that steam enthusiasts greatly admire it's the name of Scammell that always comes to mind. I expect this is because of the company's exploits with heavy haulage over the years, which again they took over from steam, even though it was very late

attraction is that many Scammells ended their days on the fairground.

In our locality on the Berkshire-Wiltshire border were the showman's firm of R Edwards and Sons, renowned country-wide for their fleet of highly-decorated and well-looked after Scammells which they travelled with their fair. The idea of having a Scammell tractor unit and lowloader to

Being stripped down for some wiring repairs, as the painting is in progress.

The wings have just been sprayed, next the cab in maroon, let's hope the cab painting goes as well as the wings.

Dragon, and things were shaping up quite nicely. We then applied a coat of varnish and, as it was drying, a cloud of thunder bugs landed on the paintwork which spoilt the end result somewhat.

It certainly looked good, and we took a photograph of it with young Frank Edwards and he said it was nearly as good as theirs. As most of the painting had been done in an open building, we moved the unit to Gordon Hedges coach station in Newbury. Here we were able to apply a good coat of varnish without the thunder bugs landing in the paintwork this had been after we had rubbed the cab down again.

The lorry was then taken to our hired barn on a local estate, where it stayed, only being used occasionally, part of the problem being we did not have the relevant driving licence. We should have taken the test! It was in 1989 that after being pestered for the Scammell father sold it to Peter Stokes, because father wanted to buy

All finished and nowhere to go. I must say she looks smart in her new livery.

Carnivals are big down in Berkshire. Here we see the Scammell Highwayman under new ownership, at least it's being used. The Scammell trailer can be seen in the background.

a Fowler traction engine which has turned out to be a financial disaster. Still that's another story, but sadly the Scammell had to go.

The new owner's mechanic Mick Watts went right through the vehicle and he even purchased the relevant Scammell lowloader to go with the unit. The trailer came from the late Jim Hutchen's collection. Peter rallied the outfit with two restored vintage tractors until the autumn of 1994, when he sold the rig to Sandy Scott of Morayshire in Scotland. So this lovely unit is now north of the border. Good luck to Sandy, he certainly has a fine Scammell. Who knows perhaps one day we will have another one, you never know. They are the Rolls-Royce of the commercial world, or are they? On that point I will leave you to ponder!

WHEELS OF ART

SCAMMELL POWER

Mike Jeffries, one-time lorry driver turned transport artist, writes about one of his favourite marques but admits to never having had the privilege of driving a Scammell...yet!

Scammell tradition goes right back to the early Victorian era when the founder, wheelwright George Scammell began coach-building vehicle bodies for horse-drawn carts and vans.

By 1916 the firm were well-known as agents and repairers of Foden and Sentinel steam wagons, also internal combustion-engined Commer Cars which were commercial vehicle manufacturers despite the name. Scammell were based at Fashion Street, Spitalfields, in the East End of London.

The Great War had demonstrated the

Below, unlike most other lorry manufacturers Scammell produced the complete articulated vehicle, designed for the most part to operate permanently coupled and the 1931 articulated eight-wheeler shown here in the livery of MRS (Marston Road Services) falls into this category. The bow front of the semi-trailer maximised the load-space and the sloping cab-back gave clearance on slopes. Chain-drive and the Gardner 6LW diesel engine were in the specification, although the 80bhp petrol-guzzling four-cylinder Scammell engine was an option. There were still no front brakes to retard up to 20 tons gross weight. The balloon tyres make a marked contrast to the narrow solids common a few years previously and the 1930s were to see great strides in lorry development unmatched since.

The frameless tanker was developed to reduce unladen weight further by dispensing with a chassis for the trailer and having the tank double as a container and support for the load. This 1926 model was built for Viners & Long who were one of the first in the field in the bulk transport of milk by road. Although transit time by rail was much quicker not all dairies were connected directly to a railhead, so costly trans-shipment made road haulage a viable alternative. The road journey from Frome in 1926 was at an average speed of 11mph - the maximum permitted speed of a solid tyred lorry was 12mph. In time road transport would take all the milk traffic in Britain from the railways. The Editor knows from his personal experience that flat out and without a trailer these Scammells would do 17mph.

potential of the motor lorry and a few years after the Armistice in 1922 the firm built a new factory at Tolpits Lane in Watford specifically for the production of their new matched articulated vehicle which was enjoying good sales. This lorry was first tested in prototype form in 1920 and featured the fifth wheel turntable which was sprung-mounted directly on to the back axle of the tractor unit. This method relieved the tractor's chassis of the weight of the front end of the semi-trailer which was, of course, carried by the rear wheels of the tractor via the turntable. The tractor chassis as a result needed only to support its own weight on relatively light springs.

At this time, because of the unclear definition of its legal status, the artic was an attractive alternative for hauliers because of

The rigid Scammell six-wheeler 6 x 2 of the early 30s was originally chain-drive and featured a dash mounted petrol tank. Later models like this box van bodied example of the Post Office Supplies Department had a live axle with bevel-drive and a conventionally placed fuel tank that now held diesel for the Gardner 6LW oil unit, as they were called all those years ago. With a six-speed constant mesh gearbox, rubber rear suspension and the very advanced feature of air-assisted brakes, they were formidable machines and many lasted into the 50s on trunk work. The last ones were swept away by the Construction and Use regulations of the mid-sixties.

its ability to carry at least a third more weight than a rigid four-wheeler without exceeding the legal maximum axle load on any one axle, and the Scammell's low unladen weight gave it even more of an advantage.

The sales success of the early models, backed up by sound engineering and innovation, was the basis for the reputation Scammell gained which was to become second to none in the transport world. The frameless tanker in 1926, the suspension system of the cross-country Pioneer chassis in 1927, which went down so well particularly with the military and the three-wheeled mechanical horse of 1933 were all firsts from Scammell. The company were also the largest trailer manufacturer in Europe, making their name one of the most respected world-wide.

The military Scammell 6 x 4 heavy recovery tractor first produced in 1939 was based on the versatile Pioneer chassis, the prototype of which dated from 1927. For heavy duty cross-country work getting on for 1,500 were provided for the armed forces between 1939 and 1946. They performed sterling work in all theatres of war.

A heavy-duty crane was fitted and a box at the front of the radiator held detachable ballast weights (removed on this example of the 6th Armoured Division). The 'coffee-pot' Pioneers (so named because of the large raised central water pot on the special pattern Still radiator to maintain the water level when the vehicle tilted) were used for many years after the war by both the military and civilian fleets as breakdown trucks or, in today's parlance, wreckers.

Scammell by any measure was a company ahead of the rest, particularly in the 1930s when one thinks of the special tankers produced for the Anglo-Iranian Oil Company in 1935 which were at least 25 years ahead of their time. In a sane world they would still be up there with the leaders. The demise and final closure in 1988 is a sad ending to a story where take-over mania and international accountancy triumphed over sound business sense and good honest engineering.

Below, the classic layout of the normal control Scammell as a tractive unit was to last until 1970 when it succumbed to fashion to be replaced by a forward-control unit. Scammell was taken over by Leyland Motors (not yet British Leyland) in 1955 and the bonneted tractor was named the Highwayman in 1958, now with the option of the 11.3 litre Leyland 0.680 engine. This late model with wrap around screen has a Gardner 6LX under its handsome bonnet and is paired with a 30ton drop frame semi-trailer with detachable rear axles to facilitate loading. In this final form and fitted with mod-cons it could probably rival any modern vehicle for comfort and looks.

Above, Gardner-engined 8 x 2 rigids were produced from 1935 and changed very little in appearance or for that matter specification until replaced by the Routeman Mk1 in the late 50s. Most were fitted with Scammell's unique rubber rear suspension and many were shod with 13.50 x 16 balloon tyres, same front and rear. The close-coupled wheel-sets gave them an appearance quite unlike their contemporaries. Due to the very low unladen weight of the chassis many were fitted with tanker and box-van bodies which always made for a very impressive vehicle. The famous Fisher Renwick box-vans, nicknamed " showboats", were a sight to be seen.

Left, the Routeman Mk 11 8 x 2 made its debut in 1962 sporting the "cheesegrater" glass fibre cab designed by the Italian Michelotti, who also styled the Triumph Herald among other cars. The heavily ribbed nature of the cab made it structurally very strong and a quantum leap in looks from the old rigid eight of only a few years previously. The later Routeman Mk III 8 x 4 with Albion double-drive rear axles was the tipperman's dream and sisters of this 1973 30-tonner of ARC Roadstone can still be seen working today.

TAILPIECE

A3 size laser copies of Mike's vehicle portraits are available at £12.50 each or three for £30 including packaging and postage from Mike Jeffries, 129 Milton Street, Brixham, Devon TQ5 0AS.

SCAMMELL 6-ton SCARAB

Nick Baldwin's 6ton Scammell Scarab recently made the trip to the new Gambrinous Drivers Museum at Romedenne B5600 in south east Belgium. The museum houses lots of old Saurer brewery vehicles and is well worth a visit. The crossing was made by Stena Line ferry from Dover.

The Perkins 4.203 powered Scammell, registration 64 AN01, which was new to the RAF. It was sold in 1977 for £260 at MoD Ruddington. It has been united with an original Watneys Scammell barrel trailer which had been towed by a Scarab in the 1950s.

The whole outfit passed to Mann & Norwich Brewery in 1988, repainted in the livery of the Cottage Brewing Company of Lovington, Somerset, which sells much of its appropriately named Norman Conquest in Northern France and

Belgium.

The Scammell has a four-speed crash gearbox and, of course, the clever automatic coupling developed in the early 1930s. Its mixture of 10, 13 and 20in tyres were located by a number of companies including Kelsey Tyre Service. The trip was very successful. Photos by Andrew Moorland.

HEAVY ME

Restoring any vintage commercial can be a challenge, but the prospect of tackling a Scammell heavy haulage tractor would not be everyone's cup of tea. Having not only completed such a task, the Freer family were still not content, so they ended up restoring another. Brian Freer and his three sons certainly don't do things by halves - they even have a pair of solid-tyred 35-ton bogies to complete their spectacular outfit.

Scammells have a very special place in British transport history. They were the industry leaders in heavy haulage vehicles. Their products were a curious blend of innovative engineering and old fashioned character. Who else would have clung on to the principle of chain drive well into the post war era? The basic specification of their last 'CD' tractor closely echoed their very early motive units from the 1920s. 'DDT32' is one of the last chain drive tractors to be built, but it could easily be mistaken for a relic of the 30s era.

Scammells had a reputation for being virtually indestructible, and there was nothing to equal them for heavy haulage. Years ago they were the mainstay of virtually every specialist heavy haulage fleet. Chief Engineer O D North's ingenious designs put the Watford manufacturer in a class of its own. Such machines as the famous 'Pioneer' (Brian has one of those too!) and the 'Explorer' became legends.

The Freers are dyed-in-the-wool transport enthusiasts. Brian, 58, lives at the small Northamptonshire village of Stoke Albany near Market Harborough, where his wife Janet runs the local post office. As well as restoring old-timers, Brian earns his living as an owner/driver.

Brian (left) and his son Joe are avid Scammell fans.

These days he is content to run just one Ford Cargo tipper, subbing work from local civil engineering company Crawshaw Robbins. At one time he ran a fleet of five tippers on contract to Tarmac at Corby. These included Thames Traders, Ford D series and a rather rare Albion Cameronian eight wheeler. The latter was basically an RE29T Super Reiver with a second steer axle added.

In the early 70s he decided to progress on to low loader work and started with an AEC Mercury Ergomatic. He soon moved up the weight scale and into Scammells. His first was a 1974 Michelotti-cabbed Handyman with a 180 Gardner. His next purchase was an ex-Shell Trunker which served him well, but there was still a need to move further up the weight scale, so Brian decided to try his luck with a Crusader. His first was a bit unusual in that it had a York trailing axle conversion. Basically, it was an ex-North Western British Road Services 4x2 tractor with a 290 Rolls but, at a quick glance, it resembled one of the heavier 6x4s, one of which was to be his next acquisition.

'UYL814S' was an 8V-71 Detroit Diesel 2-stroke Crusader 6x4 which was originally new to Pickfords Heavy Haulage, and it was a first class machine for tackling the heavier jobs up to 60 tons gtw. The Detroit was uprated to 320bhp. His final tractor before pulling out of the heavy haulage business was a 'high datum' Roadtrain 6x2, proudly bearing the Scammell name badge.

Brian's interest in old wagons began while he was still at school. He became fascinated by the many long-distance lorries which used to pass through the village on the A427, many of which were steel wagons en route to and from Stewarts & Lloyds at Corby. Other regulars were the Foden eight wheelers of Wellington Tube and AEC Mammoth Majors and Leyland Octopuses of the London Brick Company. Thousands of tons of bricks were needed for the massive rebuilding programme in Coventry following the World War II bombing raids. Brian's love of lorries was further kindled by the fact that his father was a driver at Tarmac.

His real fascination was for the abnormal load outfits which sometimes had to pass through Stoke Albany, and he vividly remembers one exciting incident when Wynns' Pacific 'Helpmate' and a Diamond T found the steep climb out of Bram Hollow too much. Loaded to the limit with a large transformer from BTH at Rugby, the outfit was held up all day in the village until a second Diamond T could be summoned in to double-head it out of trouble.

There's nothing quite so riveting going on these days, since much of the heavy industry has closed down and the village has been by-passed, but budding truck enthusiasts of the 90s can at least catch the odd glimpse of the Freer Scammells as they trundle off to rallies.

Dabbling with things mechanical comes naturally to Brian. His first venture into preservation was in 1966 when he bought an old Marshall 1220 farm tractor to restore. Shortly afterwards he bought a petrol-engined Leyland Cub breakdown truck which had started life as a furniture van but had been converted to a recovery vehicle for use by the local Co-op to tow in electric milk floats when they ran out of puff.

With an eye for rare machinery, Brian's next acquisition was a 1951 Unipower Hannibal with a Gardner 5LW. It had worked with G Walker of Syston Timber Haulage and, apart from the winch, which he described as 'done in', it was a relatively straightforward restoration job. Brian still has it and, as it stands out in the open, it is ready for a second restoration. But the Freer collection doesn't end there. Next to the Unipower stands a classic Scammell Pioneer SB25 breakdown wagon which has been used in earnest on numerous

The Highwayman 60 ton tractor has a Leyland Power Plus 680 under the bonnet.

occasions and is still capable of recovery work. This was Brian's first vintage Scammell but he later bought an ex-Pickfords Junior Constructor which had been converted to a recovery vehicle.

In his pursuit of old Scammells, he began searching for one of the classic 45-ton Chain Drives which had always held a special fascination for him. In 1984 his dreams came true. He spotted an advertisement in 'Steaming' magazine. Gerry Procter of Grewelthorpe, Boroughbridge in Yorkshire, was selling a 1946 model which had been new to showman Ted Harniess of Doncaster, and carried chassis number 1959. The last 'CD' to be built was chassis number 1963. Although designed as heavy haulage tractors, the latter 'CDs' were too outdated for such work but found a suitable role with travelling showmen.

Though DDT32 started life as a fairly standard spec CD tractor, the showman had carried out some major mods over the years to suit his own operations and, perhaps more importantly, to get it through the MoT test. The braking system

The Scammell duo on parade at Stoke Albany.

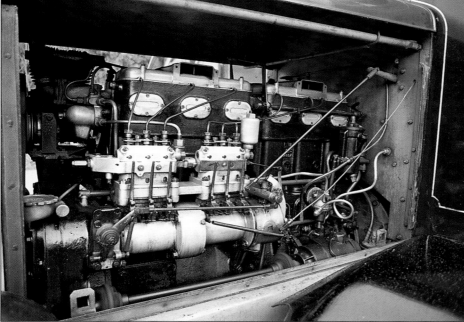

A trusty Gardner 6LW powers the old Chain Drive.

had been extensively re-worked. CDs only had brakes operating on the rear wheels but DDT32 had been fitted with a front axle from a Thornycroft Nubian which had air operated brakes. There was also a 'dead man' valve fitted to the steering column to operate the band brake on the transmission. In addition, an air servo 'booster' had been fitted into the handbrake linkage.

Clearly some sort of compromise had to be reached in order to restore some degree of authenticity without losing the benefits of the more efficient braking performance. The Thornycroft axle offended Brian's expert eye, so he set out to locate the original axle. Surprisingly it had survived in the hands of the same vendor, but before Brian could secure it, it had been earmarked for auction. Consequently he

had to bid for it and finally, some 12 months after buying the tractor, he became the proud owner of the axle for £75.

When the tractor came out of showland use it had a ballast block and a heavy duty fifth wheel coupling of unusual design, presumed to be from the Thornycroft Nubian. Prior to that the showman had fitted it with a large generator which was driven through a jack shaft off the diff. The standard 10-ton winch, date stamped 1941, is now in perfect working order following a thorough overhaul.

Remarkably enough, the cab is completely original and has survived in very sound condition. The ballast box now fitted had to be built from scratch and fitted in place of the offending fifth wheel. "The steel angle for the ballast box came from an old Boulton & Paul aircraft hangar

The two authentic 35 ton Crane bogies are ex-Pickfords.

which was being demolished at Desford airfield," explains Brian, "so it's about the right period!"

Brian believes in a no-nonsense treatment for restored commercials. He likes them to look as if they are ready to do a day's work. This is a view shared by his three sons who are 'chips off the old block'. They are all interested or involved in transport. The eldest is 35-year-old Jim who drives a Leyland DAF85 eight-wheeler for a local company called Wheelers, while 26-year-old Ben drives an Iveco Cargo six wheeled tipper for Crawshaw Robbins. He learned to drive in the Territorial Army and has held an HGV

The CD's cab interior is positively archaic by today's standards.

The CD drive has two ratios, selected by a lengthy procedure of swapping over cogs and shortening the chains.

Starting the old Gardner on the handle takes a lot of muscle.

Seventeen years separate these two giants from the Watford factory.

licence since he was 18.

Brian's other son, Joe, 31, who has his own pipe-fitting company, is the official owner of the other Scammell tractor, 579EYO. It is planned to re-instate the full Pickfords livery on this, which will mean the removal of the Aveling Barford horse emblem from the radiator grille and painting the shunt bar black. At some stage the original radiator side plates have been replaced by those from a 'box wing' model, so Joe and Brian are on the look-out for a plain pair to improve the appearance.

The tractor 579EYO was one of three Highwayman heavy duty 60-ton gtw

machines built for Pickfords Heavy Haulage in 1963. They are thought to have been referred to as 'Super Highwayman' tractors and were based at various heavy haulage depots including Walsall and Enfield. Fleet number M3023's last job, according to a movement order discovered in the cab, was transporting a steam generator from Robey's of Lincoln to Grimsby.

The tractor's specification comprises a Leyland P680 Power Plus engine with SCG (Self Changing Gears) 5-speed semi-automatic transmission driving the traditional epicyclic double reduction Scammell rear axle with a 9.4:1 ratio. 579EYO's top speed of around 35mph contrasts with the rather more modest 18mph of its chain drive ancestor.

When the Freer entourage sets out on vintage road runs it does so in style, with two genuine ex-Pickfords 35-ton 16-wheel bogies which Brian tracked down in 1988 at the well known heavy haulage specialist, Hills of Botley. The solid tyred bogies each tare at around 4.5 tons and are designed for a maximum speed of 12mph. They were built in 1958 by Cranes of Dereham.

Brian and Joe had a stark reminder of the bogies' speed limitations when they tried pulling them at 30mph to attend the 1996 Classic Commercial Motor Show at Rugby. One of the wheel bearings seized and it was a while before they realised that

Scammell - a proud British name synonymous with strength and durability.

the solid tyres on that axle were being worn down to a flat. Such items are difficult to find and expensive to replace so great caution now has to be exercised to avoid it happening again.

Soon after restoring EYO, Brian and Joe were contacted by one of Pickfords' men, who used to drive its sister vehicle 578EYO, Fleet No M3022. John Carpenter, who has been retired for some years, spent his whole career in heavy haulage, as did his father before him, going right back to the days of steam haulage with Norman Box.

Just recently, Brian's vintage fleet has been added to yet again. His latest acquisition is, somewhat surprisingly, not a Scammell but an AEC. In a bid to achieve something completely different, he has purchased a completely derelict 1939 AEC Mammoth Minor 366L. The rare machine is currently undergoing a complete rebuild and we can rest assured that when it emerges from the Freer workshop (hopefully, I am told, some time next year) it will be 100% authentic and, like the Scammells, looking ready for a day's work.

On Location
with Peter Davies

This month Peter Davies captures on film two heavy haulage ex-Pickfords Scammells, which are seen powering their way along the road. The 60ton Highwayman leading the 45ton CD of father and son outfit Brian and Joe Freer.

OLD GRANNY

A welcome addition to the restoration fleet!

By Bill Robins

A lot of Scammells have survived to preservation but they are mostly the big heavy haulage versions. It was nice to come across a Crusader restored to perfection like this one.

HMA 468N, chassis number GHV 59040, was originally new to ICI's Mond division at Northwich, Cheshire, and wore the fleet number 68. It was found, along with some more of the same, in a breaker's yard in north Lincolnshire, and purchased for restoration by the present owner Majid Shamsa, or Jid as he likes to be known. Jid came to this country from Persia (now called Iran) in 1959, got married, and has lived here ever since. He runs a furniture import business running Scanias from his base on an airfield in north Lincolnshire and imports several loads of furniture a week from as far afield as Romania and Slovenia, as well as taking out general cargo to almost anywhere in Europe and then loading back with his own goods for

The cab interior looks superb and has been cleaned and rebuilt to perfection.

The stainless steel exhaust system is an interesting addition to the vehicle's looks.

home. The high standard of restoration in the Crusader is to the same standard as his road going lorries - how many people can boast of a customised Scania 143 as a spare motor? The trailers are all kitted out with extra marker lights and extra rear lights as well, and one of Shamsa's lorries looks a treat coming down the road.

The restoration of the Crusader took four years to complete, as it was a chassis-upwards rebuild. The cab was very badly rotted, which is no surprise, as most Motor Panels cabs have gone the same way, and it

was decided to take it off the chassis so the extent of the rot could be seen and treated. All the rotten tinwork was replaced and great pains were taken to keep everything looking original and 'right' as far as possible. Although not a tilt cab, the Crusader had a hinged radiator which swung out to give access to the front of the engine, which made life a little easier than a fixed cab for maintenance work. The engine, which is a Rolls-Royce Eagle 290 turbocharged unit, came out along with the Fuller nine-speed RTO9509A

You could well imagine the Crusader touring weekly to the continent with the Sharma trailer.

overdrive gearbox, and they were both worked on very heavily during the restoration.

The original upright exhaust was replaced with an Eminox which, while perhaps not in keeping with the originality theme, will not need replacing for a long time! Eminox also made up the stack for the air cleaner inlet. The original fifth wheel coupling has been retained and it is one of those 'two handed jobs' which were guaranteed to get black grease on you before you had started work. While the engine and gearbox were receiving attention, the chassis was taken down the road to be shot blasted and to receive its first coat of primer paint.

Once the engine and gearbox were back in the chassis, the whole lot was treated to the same paint job as Shamsa's road going lorries, and work began on the trimming of the cab interior. No customisation here, it's been replaced exactly as it was, and Jid even gave up the idea of running the Crusader on local

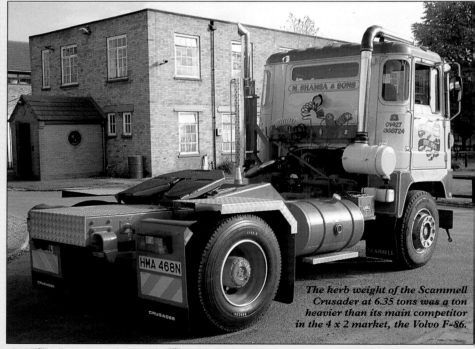

The kerb weight of the Scammell Crusader at 6.35 tons was a ton heavier than its main competitor in the 4 x 2 market, the Volvo F-86.

There were no less than 22 prototype Crusaders that were tested by BRS before the final design was accepted.

work when he realised that he'd have to fit a tachograph, which would have ruined the look of the interior.

While I was taking the photos for this article, Jid was having great fun posing with the Crusader and, with the Eminox stack, it sounded terrific - a rattle from the bottom end and a roar from the top! This vehicle has gone over so well it could go back to work tomorrow and not look amiss on the road of today.

HMA 468N joins several other restored vehicles that are owned by Jid, these being a 1954 5ton Albion that used to belong to Yorkshire Copper at Barrhead, also a 1950 Austin van which was once an ambulance, and a couple of motorbikes. The Albion is due to take part in the HCVS London to Brighton run in 1998, and it looks every bit as good as the Crusader, so watch out for it!

Below, the older vehicles in the Shamsa fleet, the 1950 Austin Loadstar and the Albion Chieftain, are seen resting peacefully.

VETERANS' REUNION

By Peter Davies

It is not often that an owner is re-united with his old lorry from nearly half a century ago but that is the case with Roy Woodcock and his Bedford Scammell OSS artic. The 1948 Bedford was unearthed at a scrapyard in Bythorn near Molesworth, Cambridgeshire in 1994 and has since undergone a complete rebuild. It is now back in perfect working order and finished in the smart blue and red livery of the current Woodcock fleet.

Roy and his two sons, Brian and David, run a long established family haulage business based at Ampthill in Bedfordshire - the county where the lorry was built and from which it takes its name. Back in the 40s and 50s Bedford O types were an indispensable part of the UK transport scene and many firms built their success on the low cost petrol engined workhorses.

Roy recalls how his father Bob came to

Trevor Stringer's artistic skills came in handy in recreating a Scammell grille badge.

Seventy five year old Roy Woodcock has spent his whole life in road haulage.

The 'OSS' was a joint product of Vauxhall Motors and Scammell Lorries.

purchase EJU898 from the old BRS depot in Dean Street, Bedford when it closed down in the mid fifties. The truck was new to Frederick Riley of Melton Mowbray on 1st January 1948. Just one year later it changed ownership to haulage contractors T & R J Mackley of Harrison Road, Leicester who were nationalised in October 1949, becoming Unit E42 of the Road Haulage Executive (the RHE was the official title of the BRS controlling body). Subsequent changes recorded on the original log book during its time with BRS include South Leicester Group, Blaby (E41), which was under the management of the well known Miss A M Walker, and a change of address to Harborne Road, Edgbaston, Birmingham - the BRS Midlands Divisional Headquarters - in 1953. In its latter days with BRS it was based at Bedford.

Whilst with British Road Services the Bedford was finished in Road Service Green livery with black chassis and red wheels, and operated with a 20ft, 8-ton payload Scammell trailer. While such vehicles were generally used on short haul local traffic, EJU is believed to have frequently made trips to Birmingham with bricks, usually back-loading steel for the Bedfordshire and London areas.

Traditional style signwriting sets the finished truck off nicely.

Cab interior is spot on and totally in character.

Roy had the honour of collecting the Bedford from the BRS sale and he was to become its driver for the first few weeks. It was the first artic to join the fleet. Eventually it was to put in about 13 years' service and for most of that time it was driven by Gordon Owen who gave forty years loyal service to Woodcock's, having joined the firm in the late 30s. Sadly, Gordon died a couple of years ago before he could witness the rebuild of his old wagon.

It was by sheer chance that Roy, now 75, discovered the long lost truck. He had already rebuilt a Bedford QL as a nostalgic reminder of his four and a half years army service during the war. He served in the Royal Army Ordnance Corps in the Middle East, Italy and Sicily and had fond memories of the famous QL 4x4s. It was in 1987 that he decided to buy one for restoration - a task which was to take three years. He rebuilt it from scrap condition, returning it to its original military spec exactly as it appeared in war-time service. It was a very early example from the first year of production.

During a visit to Joe Hunt's yard at Bythorn in 1994 to search for QL bits the subject of Bedford Scammell artics came up. Joe recalled taking in such a machine many years earlier. It was virtually buried under other scrap but when it was pulled out Roy could hardly believe his eyes - it turned out to be the very vehicle that his father had bought from BRS back in 1955.

He had last seen it when it was given 'on permanent loan' to a farmer at Cranfield in 1968, having become outmoded for haulage work. The new owner had used it in and around the farm but eventually it was laid up and allowed to deteriorate. In 'as found' condition

the Bedford could best be described as derelict, the cab having gone missing. Roy was only able to recognise it from certain tell-tale features such as welded repairs he had carried out himself. What confirmed it was the front nearside spring - just a few days before it was withdrawn from service he had fitted a new one. He had been able to put in a new shackle pin at the rear but there wasn't a front pin available so he replaced the old one. Sure enough, the front nearside spring on the scrapped machine showed no sign of the usual wear on the underside of the leaves. Also the front pin was well worn compared with the rear.

Having positively identified the chassis as that of EJU, Roy did a deal with Joe Hunt and

Old A licences add a nice touch.

collected the rusting remains on one of his modern artics. Four and a half years and much blood, sweat and tears later, the Bedford is back to her old self. It was quite a daunting task refurbishing the truck but all the effort has been worth while. The restoration has been carried out to an excellent standard and Roy has resisted any temptation to bull the vehicle up unrealistically. The result is a period style working lorry that would completely blend in to a 1960's traffic scene.

Unfortunately the '28 horse' six-cylinder petrol engine was too far gone to be worth overhauling so a replacement was obtained from Bedford enthusiast Barry Webb at Duxford. It is a civilian spec engine and came out of a low mileage airport fire truck. Records show that it had been overhauled in 1953 by Vauxhall Motors Ltd. Although it was in reasonably good condition it needed some major work to get it going - a local engine reconditioning firm, JPDT Trading at Flitwick, was called upon to make new valve guides and seats as both were badly corroded. It now runs well and is returning about 12mpg.

The cover plate was missing from the diff housing as were some of the diff components, so Roy decided to take the opportunity to install a replacement diff of a higher ratio which gives the

Originally Vauxhall Motors built the chassis, Scammell supplied and fitted the coupling.

truck a bit more speed as well as improving economy. OSS models (which incidentally stands for O type Short wheelbase, Scammell coupling) were fitted with a 7.4:1 ratio as standard since they were designed for an 8-ton payload (12 tons gross) while the normal O type truck for 4/5-ton payload had a 6.4:1 ratio. Now EJU has a 6.4:1 diff fitted and is capable of about 40mph although a comfortable cruising speed is 35.

During the process of restoration Roy also decided to make some improvements to the braking system - something he had intended to do back in the 60s but had never got round to it! Now, thirty years on, he has finally realised his plans. On the basic OSS artic the tractor brakes

relied on leg power operating a dual circuit hydraulic system while a vacuum servo, actuated by a valve incorporated into the footbrake linkage, worked the trailer brakes. The trailer servo on EJU had been smashed by the sheer weight of the scrap above it, so prompting the major rework. Roy's modifications meant incorporating a QL vacuum servo into the tractor system, dispensing with the existing trailer valve and piping the vacuum to the trailer servo via the tractor servo.

Apparently the brakes are now brilliant - far better than they were in the original set up. Roy points out that the old theory of applying more braking effort to the trailer axle to reduce the risk of jack-knifing was found to be flawed. New thinking surfaced during the 60s suggesting that artics were more stable when braking was increased on the tractor front axle.

Getting the right sort of cross ply tyres is not so easy nowadays but Roy was lucky enough to round up a nice set of 7.00x20s with an appropriate tread pattern. Fitted to the correct pattern of 8-stud 20in. centres, they add to the vehicle's authentic appearance. The cab itself is spot on too but Roy had to do a lot of tricky welding to bring it up to its present condition. The wings had rotted away in several places. As the original cab had gone missing Roy had to

locate a suitable cab of the correct 1948 pattern and once again Barry Webb came to the rescue. One of the biggest problems turned out to be finding a good pair of windscreens. Another item which has proved impossible to find is a genuine 'Scammell' grille badge but his lorry enthusiast friend Trevor Stringer, who once drove for Woodcock's, has made a very convincing replica which is hard to tell from the real thing.

The 6 volt electrical system has been fully converted to 12 volt to give improved performance and meticulous attention has been paid to fitting the correct type of headlamps with their distinctive lens pattern. The headlamp glasses were obtained from an enthusiast in Devon. The TK style flashers are exactly the type that a haulier would have added during the 60s when they became necessary items. Inside the cab the seating has been re-upholstered in the characteristic green 'rexine' type material and the general interior finish is exactly how it would have appeared on a working lorry during the 50s and 60s era.

Of course a tractor unit is not much good without a suitable trailer so Roy was delighted when a genuine Scammell automatic coupling van trailer turned up at a yard in Sussex. He would not have found it but for the fact that its owners had bought one of Woodcock's Volvo F7s. When they noticed he was restoring the OSS tractor they asked if he was interested in a Scammell box trailer, so they did a deal. It is actually quite a bit later than the unit and dates from the early 60s. It once operated with the well known Charles Kinloch grocery fleet and has the added bonus of a tail lift. Roy jokes that as he and his wife get older the tail lift comes in very useful for getting in and out of the trailer which serves as an ideal living van at rallies!

The modern artics in Woodcock's current fleet are a far cry from the type of truck Roy's father started with back in late 20s. That truck was a left hand drive Model T and was used to cart vegetables to the London markets, usually backloading groceries for local retail stores. Nowadays the firm operates six artics including two Scanias, two MANs and two Volvo F10s. There are also an Iveco Ford Cargo 7.5 tonner and a Transit on the fleet. Much of the traffic consists of plastics products for a large local manufacturer but bricks and general goods are also carried.

Looking back to the early days Roy's father, Bob (Robert David Woodcock), was temporarily forced to lay up his truck during the worst of the 30s depression and to take a driving job at the London Brick Company. There he drove AEC Mammoth Major MK.II eight wheelers. At that time they had the early Ricardo head diesel which was difficult to start on cold mornings. Roy recalls how the burning rag treatment was called for while the finger was kept firmly pressed on the starter button. Bob was pleased when he was given the job of driving the LBC's first direct injection AEC which was a great advance.

Bob started back on his own with an old Commer Centaur in 1941. By the end of the war he owned four wagons including a Bedford OW 5-ton tipper which was used to deliver coal from Ampthill station to various local factories. After the war he bought some

Automatic trailer coupling was a boon for quick turnaround on local work.

ex-War Dept Commers and converted them to dual rear wheels. From about 1950 he started carting bricks as there was enormous demand with the construction of Stevenage New Town and the expansion of Hemel Hempstead. All such traffic was closely regulated as, during nationalisation, private hauliers were restricted to a 25 mile radius on a B licence.

As haulage was partly de-nationalised from 1953 Bob bought an ex-BRS Dennis Pax and a Bedford OLB 5-tonner on a special A licence. During the 50s he bought out a couple of local hauliers to gain more A licences and the fleet gradually expanded. Larger premises were purchased at Chandos Road in Ampthill in the mid 50s. At one stage there were ten lorries on the fleet including Bedford S-types and Commer QXs. Roy himself began work in the garage at London Brick in 1937 when he was just 14. He went on to driving by the time he was 18. One of the first wagons he drove was a petrol engined Leyland Cub.

He served in the Army from 1941 until 1946 and after demob he joined his father in the haulage business which he eventually took over and has run ever since. Nowadays he likes a quiet life and leaves a lot of the hard work to his sons, Brian (50) and David (48). Even so he still keeps his hand in and thinks nothing of taking a load down to the west country in the Cargo 7.5 tonner. Obviously Roy Woodcock is not one to be idle - when not helping to keep the modern fleet rolling he is busy looking after his much cherished Bedford Scammell. The old timer is a real credit to a true haulage man, but he modestly asks that some of that credit should go to his fellow enthusiast Barry Webb and the many other people who have helped him to complete the difficult task of restoration. ●

The O type was probably Bedford's most famous truck of all time.

New Restorations Star at the Scammell Gathering,
May 10 1998. Alec Kermotschuk
visited the event.

SCAMMELL GATHE

T he Scammell Gathering was held near junction 38 on the M1, on the A637, which is signposted for Huddersfield. The rally was open to owners and enthusiasts of Scammells and other makes.

The event was organised by Alan and Christine Rogerson of Hemsworth and was a very laid back and a casual affair, with no marshals as such and certainly no entry fee! Nevertheless, the purpose of the event was to raise money, by way of donations, for Cancer Research, if the public so wished. Although this was a one-day event, a good number of the entrants travelled up on the Saturday.

Those who attended included the president of the Scammell Register, Bill Brombridge, along with Jack Kimp, the

The vehicles just about filled the site and the event was a good start to the season.

The Scammell Mountaineer certainly looked a beast and is seen leaving the site on an ERF outfit.

Register's secretary. I was reminded that the Register started 15 years ago in 1983 and now has over 400 members. The organisation helps its members find parts as well as keeps them up-to-date with the Scammell scene via the regular newsletter. Members can be found in Italy, Holland and even New Zealand.

First on the scene was Paul Hicks of Leeds with his 1953 Scammell Explorer, registration MVS 863. This good looking machine did 38 years in the REME, based at Sheffield with the Royal Signals. Its markings are the original ones and are an amalgamation of the Tyne Tees and the West Yorkshire Regiment. The Scammell boasts the nickname 'Doolan Dragster', commemorating the driver of the vehicle at

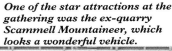

One of the star attractions at the gathering was the ex-quarry Scammell Mountaineer, which looks a wonderful vehicle.

the time, a Corporal Doolan. Paul went on to explain that, while in service, the engine blew a piston and, as a result, it was taken out of service and not repaired, and was eventually sold at auction in Hunslet, Leeds.

The organisers of the event, Alan and Christine Rogerson, brought along their two Scammells, a 1943 Pioneer YYJ 792 and a Mountaineer HRR 348D.

Also spotted were two top class recovery vehicles. One was owned locally by Alan Smith of Huddersfield, an ex-military AEC Matador, which had a crane fitted in 1969. Also looking magnificent was Glyn Heseltine's 1939 Austin K2 recovery

The mighty 1953 Scammell Explorer MVS 863 belonging to Paul Hicks of Leeds, which did 38 years of REME Service.

ING

Also seen at the event was the mighty Diamond T of Graham Booth in Pickfords livery.

The ex-Gloucestershire County Council 1963 Highwayman has been painted in the heavy haulier company of Elliot's of Rufforth, York. Without doubt it was the star attraction at the Scammell event. Its owner, David Weedon of York, has certainly done a good job of restoration.

The fifth-wheel coupling and the winch rollers are clearly seen on David Weedon's Highwayman.

Howard Waters' long wheelbase 1966 Leyland Comet, in its black livery, made an interesting addition to the ranks of preserved vehicles in recent months. This Sheffield based vehicle, registered EXJ 745D, will be featured in a future edition of Classic & Vintage Commercials.

Getting back to the Scammells; Malcolm Holder's 1967 Highwayman LHW 60E fitted with a Gardner 6LX engine, which was new to Stamps of Bristol before entering showland use, certainly stood out.

Travelling all the way from Worthing, West Sussex was John Mitchell and his 1958 Foden S20 ballast tractor, registered VWF 704 and carrying the livery of Brooksbank Haulage of Hull. John was made very welcome on his visit up north. Also enjoying the event was publicity secretary for the Scammell Register, Barry Partridge, who came up from Lancing with his Scammell Handyman towing his ex-roller living van. All in all the event was a great success and a good start to the season.

vehicle, which had taken Glyn 12 months to rebuild.

Making only its second appearance was John Dykes' 1951 Bedford K type NSJ 753. Yet another vehicle to make its debut at this event was the 1963 Scammell Highwayman tractor unit ASV 610, of David Weedon from York. This was presented in the livery of Elliot Haulage of Rufforth, near York and had been rebuilt to a high standard. The interior is to be finished off in the near future. Even the winch rope guides had been painted in aluminium paint. The Leyland 680 Power Plus sounded great, and the vehicle was brought to the event on David's lowloader.

Making its second appearance since restoration was the 1951 Bedford KC of John Dykes, which looked the part.

SCAMMELL GATHERING

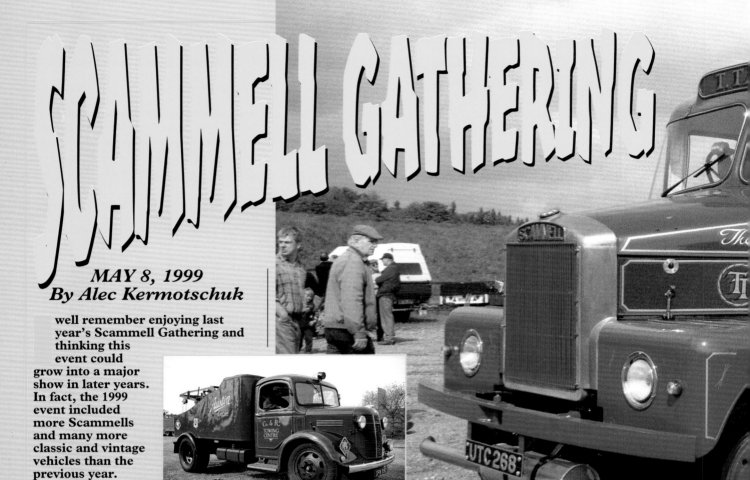

MAY 8, 1999
By Alec Kermotschuk

well remember enjoying last year's Scammell Gathering and thinking this event could grow into a major show in later years. In fact, the 1999 event included more Scammells and many more classic and vintage vehicles than the previous year. What's more, I can foresee next year's gathering being even larger, as it will be moved from the present location just off the M1 at junction 38 to the village of Ackworth.

This is largely due to the fact that the present site is not big enough for the growing number of exhibits, and public parking is somewhat restricted. We will keep you informed of the changes. However, back to this year's show, and what a great day it turned out to be. The sun was shining and there were plenty of classic and vintage commercials to look at, along with a good number of trade stands.

According to organisers, Alan and Christine Rogerson, you can never be sure exactly what's going to turn up. This means it's even more exciting, as there's no set programme, just a casual affair with people enjoying themselves among this splendid turnout of vehicles. The Scammell Register's president,

Glyn Heseltine of Barnsley with his superb Austin K2 recovery truck.

Seen reversing into position is Tommy Taylor of Warrington and his splendid 1950 Highwayman with Gardner 180 engine. It was Tommy's first time at this event.

Smaller than most of the Scammells at the event, John Baxter's Scammell Scarab was new in 1959 to Cadburys, working in the tinner's yard till 1976.

Looking very smart is Paul Hammond's 1958 ex-Pickfords Scammell Junior Constructor, which took the best part of five years to restore.

Another Highwayman from John Myers' stable is this 1964 example, finished in the very smart green livery of Isaac Timmins.

Bill Brombridge and the secretary, Jack Kimp were present to chat with members old and new about their experiences of owning and restoring Scammell lorries.

It always amazes me when people I talk to travel literally hundreds of miles to be at these events, such is the spirit of these dedicated enthusiasts. One such person was Paul Hammond of Pangbourne in Berkshire, who travelled the best part of 200 miles with his Volvo FH12 and low loader. On the back was his very smart 1958 Scammell Junior Constructor, VXD 530, in a superb BRS ex-Pickfords blue livery. The Scammell was originally based in the West Country, working for Pickfords, before being passed on to a

recovery breakdown company in Exeter. It then did some further work in the haulage business before Paul acquired M2070 in a very poor state. The wooden cab was completely rotten and had to be rebuilt, along with the ballast box. Basically it had a complete rebuild from the ground up. Although a lot of the body panels were fabricated and rebuilt, where practical, Paul did reuse original parts of the bodywork, such as the wings and doors. As for the engine and gearbox, these needed nothing more than a good overhaul. The completed project was then professionally sprayed, using a two-pack paint, and lettered. Incidentally, Peter Davies assisted Paul in recreating the original BRS

First time out for Gerry Elders and his recently restored 1964 Highwayman ballast tractor.

John Carnevale's superb 1929 Ford Model A recovery truck, fitted with a rare two-speed back axle.

emblems on the doors.

Two very interesting Scammells owned by John Myers of Huddersfield were present. CDB 666B is a 1962 Highwayman, complete with trailer in the splendid green livery of Isaac Timmins, and powered by a Leyland 680 diesel. His second outfit is a 1964 Scammell Highwayman, registered BAW 850B and powered by a Gardner 6LW - this one was complete with a trailer loaded with cable drums and finished in the dark blue livery of Wrekin Roadways.

Moving on to a smaller vehicle, and one seen at many events, is John Baxter's 1959 Scammell Scarab. This vehicle was new to Cadburys, the famous chocolate manufacturers, and used until 1976 in their tinner's yard. It then passed to a second owner, believed to be a railway society in Wales, before ending up in a scrapyard. John bought the Scarab in a very poor state in 1993 and spent the next 18 months restoring it to its present superb condition.

Andrew Reid from Doncaster brought along his fine 1961 Highwayman, registration BGO 234, which was new to Shell Petroleum before ending up in the amusement business before Andrew acquired it in 1985. He spent many

long and hard hours restoring the Highwayman back to its present condition.

A good number of Scammells do in fact end up in the recovery business, for the obvious reason that they can pull and push tremendous loads. One such example is a 1978 Crusader, owned by Steve Bullivant of Doncaster. His Scammell is in use as a recovery vehicle, and is powered by a Rolls-Royce 350 engine. Making its debut after restoration was Gerry Elder's 1964 Highwayman ballast unit, XJV 801, which travelled from Harrogate. Gerry acquired it in November last year and literally only completed the work the night before the event.

One little Scammell that created a lot of interest was a quarter scale working model based on the original full-size Scammell Mountaineer with crew cab owned by Dave Smith of Eastburn. The model is powered by a Petter single-cylinder petrol engine and was built and owned by Jack Hutchinson of Eastburn.

Scammells were not the only classic commercials present by any means. In fact, there was a good turn out of many other makes. A 'new' vehicle on the scene was the 1929 Ford Model A recovery truck, HE 6915, beautifully restored and owned by John Carnevale of Pontefract. What makes this vehicle special is that it's factory fitted with a two-speed back axle, which I'm told is quite rare. It started its working life as a gang mower for Barnsley Council and had spoked wheels at that time. Unfortunately, while in use the spokes came loose, and as a result the wheels were changed to a solid type. The little Ford changed hands a number of times until eventually John acquired it and spent the next ten years carrying out a complete chassis-up rebuild. John's brother David is also no stranger to vintage vehicle restoration, as he carried out a similar restoration project on his splendid 1928 Albion LB 40 flatbed back in 1997. Again, this work involved the complete rebuild of the body, and the original engine was replaced. Apparently it was new to a farmer in Rotherham, who used the little Albion for coal and milk deliveries. It also had a special duty during the war serving the Home Guard as a water bowser.

Another superb Albion was the 1971 Reiver fixed tipper, HAL 45K, owned by Geoff Thomas of Matlock, with its bright red cab

Steve Bristow of Howden pauses for the camera with his smart 1970 Handyman recovery vehicle in a striking bright yellow livery.

and outstanding paint job. At this event for the first time was Ray Dawson with his 1956 Ford Thames ET6 ex-police mobile column, RYX 266, powered by a 3.5-litre V8 petrol engine. New to the Home Office in London during May 1956, the same year it moved to the Civil Defence Department Police headquarters based in Glasgow. The Ford ended its working life at Ayr County Council Buildings Department in 1959 and was found by Ken Sykes in 1991, who restored the vehicle to its present condition prior to Ray becoming the owner.

Attending the gathering for the second year, Glyn Heseltine of Barnsley brought along his very smart Austin K2 recovery truck. Glyn restored the little Austin from a very poor condition over a 12 month period.

That's just a brief look at some of the many superb vehicles at the Scammell Gathering, and I hope I've whetted your appetite enough to make you go along next year. My thanks to Alan and Christine Rogerson for making me very welcome. Next year we'll see the Scammell Gathering move to Ackworth. We all look forward to that!

SCAMMELLS

Nearly finished! Ex-Gloucestershire County Council Scammell Highwayman only needs interior work and fifth wheel coupling finishing.

It's bigger and better! That's the message from the many vehicle exhibitors and spectators at the 1st Scammell & Historic Vehicle Gathering, held at Ackworth, near Pontefract in Yorkshire.

What makes this event special is that people can give a donation to Yorkshire Cancer Research.

We'd already reported that this show was growing into something big, and it certainly has done, thanks to event

organisers Alan and Christine Rogerson, and agricultural contractor Derek Bywater, who kindly provided the site and its facilities free of charge.

Committee members of both the Scammell Register and the Scammell Owners and Enthusiasts' Club were on hand to discuss various aspects of running and owning Scammell vehicles.

Phil Winterburn and his son Philip brought along not one, but two ex-Army Scammell vehicles, driving them all the way from Oldham. These vehicles don't stand idle, in fact Phil has taken the 1952

Constructor to France or Holland each year since 1989, averaging 1,500 miles a year, while Philip covers some 700 miles annually in his smart Explorer. Both vehicles are powered by Leyland 680 engines, giving a top speed of around 35mph.

Making its first rally appearance was Dave Weedon's all original Scammell Crusader, direct from military service and fitted with an EKA recovery crane, which he intends to use for his recovery business. With its Rolls-Royce 305 engine, the Scammell will prove very useful.

Just out of service is this 1980 Scammell Crusader, Rolls 350 powered, fitted with Swedish EKA recovery gear and ready for a working career with owner Dave Weeden.

Ex-Army Scammells were out in strength at the event, SSU 734, a Constructor, covers 1,500 miles a year, and also pictured is Explorer VSY 557.
Both date from 1952, are Leyland 680-powered and owned by the Winterburn family.

N SHOW
Alex Kermotschuk reports

...cammell Highwayman tractor units have beautifully ...ohn Myers of Huddersfield.

Dave also showed his very smart 1963 ...ex-Gloucester County Council Highwayman, now registered ASV 610 and painted in the bright yellow livery of Elliotts. Only interior finishing and bolting on the fifth wheel coupling is needed to finish this project.

Dave Gee of Wakefield brought along three vehicles from his highly impressive fleet including 1939 Scammell LA ballast tractor FSU 404, first seen at last year's Trans Pennine Road Run. Powered by a Gardner 6LW oil engine delivering 102bhp @ 1,700rpm through a six-speed all constant mesh gearbox, this Scammell spent much of its life at a Southampton oil refinery, and was taken out of service in the 1980s.

Thanks to David, the vehicle is now skilfully restored and painted in the distinctive colours of Gee's Haulage, being driven to the event by driver Colin Wright.

David's love of fairground organ music has inspired him to buy a Mortier Fairground Organ, fitted in a 1966 International Harvester Loadstar box lorry, this having been painted in the blue Gees livery. He has, over the past 12 months, travelled to a number of rallies with his 'Rig' as he calls it.

Dave's Volvo N10, TUA 666R, was featured in the March issue of Classic and Vintage Commercials, and he's currently tackling a Scammell Mountaineer, the ongoing restoration of which this magazine featured in May. We'll keep you informed.

Benny Harrison travelled down from County Durham in his 1971 Scammell Handyman wrecker, new to Freeway Haulage and run as an artic unit for 10 years, later passing to Thirlwell Coaches and being converted into a recovery vehicle. Benny bought the vehicle in 1998, and has carried out a complete rebuild.

"Just in the nck of time" are the words used by Nicky Sykes of Huddersfield to describe the recent restoration of his smart 1952 Unipower four-wheel-drive tractor unit, VRT 699, the rebuild of which was completed just days before the event. The work was all carried out by Nicky and a friend, Dave Jackson.

John Denning travelled down from York with his 1970 ERF LV tractor unit, RCA 267H, carrying his lovingly restored 1947 Austin dropside lorry, MSK 378.

Another rally attraction was a very rare 1948 Douglas Timber Tractor, BCF 960, brought along by owner Steve Pawson of Sheffield. New to Robert Pye of Suffolk for timber haulage, and probably fitted with an AEC engine, the Douglas now has a Leyland 400 engine driven through a six-speed gearbox, a combination increasing the top speed from 36mph to a staggering 41!

'Keeping Jazz Alive' was the unusual

Alan and Christine Rogerson's 1966 Scammell Mountaineer Ballast Box vehicle was restored in an open shed at the side of their house. It's in the livery of original owners the Foraky Drilling Co.

First time out following restoration, this 1952 Gardner 4LW-powered Unipower was finished in the nick of time for the event

message on an extremely smart 1967 Scammell Highwayman, owned by the Day family from Staffordshire.

This has been modified with power steering, a high ratio differential and an air suspended driver's seat, all to give better comfort when travelling to gigs - the family are all members of the Canal Stompers jazz band!

*Event organisers Alan and Christine would like to thank Highway Recovery Milnes House Securities and Traffic Management Services for their help and assistance.

Steve Pawson's rare 1948 Douglas Timber Tractor was supplied new to Robert Pye of Suffolk.

34 years old and still working - this 1966 Highwayman of S Harrison & Sons is approaching i

THE GATHERINGS:
SCAMMELL

*Alec Kermotschuk at the Scammell and Historic Vehicle Gathering,
Ackworth, nr Pontefract*

Something for all enthusiasts could be found among the good turn-out of Scammells at this event... held in aid of cancer research.

Explorers, Crusaders, Pioneers, Mountaineers, Highwaymans (or is it Highwaymen?) and even a Routeman with a 1970s Michelotti-designed glassfibre cab in a striking yellow livery, brought along by the Bristow family of Howden, near Goole.

Scammell King Dave Gee even brought along his ex-Wynns Mountaineer (or was it? - wait and see for future instalments of this vehicle's restoration in *CVC*), showing off its new and skilfully crafted ash-cab frame.

Dave always brings along something special, this year surprising the spectators with a very rare 1942 Scammell Fire Trailer Pump, towed on the back of his Land Rover.

New on the scene and looking superb - in fact still smelling of fresh paint - was NGF 875, a 1953 Type-15 MU in the green and red livery of TD Cotterill of Silkstone Common. This vehicle has certainly had the treatment, a complete chassis - upwards rebuild by Ian Moore Motor Bodies of Burnley, Lancs. A second MU present, belonging to George Strutt of Darley Dale, recently starred in the TV series *Peak Practice*.

Ex-Sunters Super Constructor, 447

Work is definitely cracking ahead on Dave Gee's Scammell Mountaineer. More on this vehicle in future issues.

*Soon to be stripped down and rebuilt by owner Dave W
is this 1958 ex-Sunters Scammell Constructor.*

h mile.

This 1957 MU recently appeared in the TV series Peak Practice.

THE GATHERINGS
SCAMMELL
EX KERMOTSCHUK REPORTS

OPY, powered by a 250 Cummins engine, attended the event on a low loader. Owner David Weedon, from York, intends to strip it down and carry out a full chassis - up rebuild this year.

S Harrison & Sons of Tinsley, Sheffield, showed a 1966 Highwayman, LWJ 473D, still in use after 34 years, having covered the best part of two million miles.

This event had started as a small gathering of Scammells, but has now grown into a full-scale classic vehicle rally, with a fine selection of Dennis fire engines among the other exhibits.

No Scammell rally could be complete without a herd of Mechanical Horses. This example, owned by Terry Jordan, has been rebuilt. It's now in Jordan Transporters livery.

Another surprise from Scammell King Dave Gee was this extremely rare Scammell Fire Hose Pump, previously belonging to rally organiser Alan Rogerson.

You could still smell the paint drying on this superb Type-15 MU, which has just undergone a chassis - up rebuild by Ian Moore Motor Bodies of Burnley.

As a young lad brought up in the small Norfolk town of Loddon, the excitement and anticipation of the arrival of Gray's of Thurston's fair still lives with me today. The fair was set up on Church Plain, an open space facing the primary school.

Chasing in and around the trucks, living vans and rides during playtime before and after school was as much part of the experience as riding on the dodgems and gallopers with Mum and Dad.

The roar of the generators and the smell of diesel from ERFs, ex-World War Two Mack tractors and of course the Scammells, was a heady cocktail, and I promised myself then that one day, somehow, I must become a proud owner.

I couldn't believe my luck when there in the February 98 edition of *Old Glory* magazine was a small ad from Benny Irvin, "Scammell for sale". My first skirmish with Benny Irvin was not a success, he wanted too much money for what appeared to be a rather decrepit truck! However, I sent my friend Stuart Heath along with cash in hand, and the deal was done!

The truck arrived back at Stuart's yard, Bodycraft of Rudgwick, where the Scammell was completely stripped for sand blasting. The 6LW Gardner engine was shipped to Walsh Engineering in Manchester for a complete rebuild. Nearby Vintage Wings Ltd crafted a full new set of wings, while the tyres were sent away for remoulding.

The cab presented the greatest challenge as rust and rot had taken their toll over the years, ruling out the possibility of repair.

A John Butler picture of the Irvin outfit seen about to depart Botany car park, Tonbridge, Kent. The Scammell is to the left of the picture and was notorious for poor brakes. At various times of the year the Botany car park housed some wonderful commercial vehicles which were a delight to the handful of vehicle enthusiasts in the area, young and old. A small proportion have been restored.

Stuart knew of a lad who had made very professional ash frames for vintage cars, and we were soon to have Trevor Coldman and his metal bashing colleague Steve Denyer on the case. Very careful measurements and notes were taken of the original and work commenced. ●

Continued next month

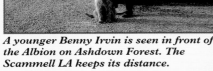

A younger Benny Irvin is seen in front of the Albion on Ashdown Forest. The Scammell LA keeps its distance.

The old girl looks a bit tired after moving some mountains in her time.

The Scammell arrives in Sussex! Run for your lives as the tractor unit hurries down the ramps.

It's time to start dismantling the Scammell as the works dog comes to join the fun!

The Gardner 6LW which Benny wanted to fire up and drive on to the low loader. Just as well that we refused as Walsh's found all the main bearings were completely shot!

MAN
STRY

about his fabulous 1942
ll LA tractor.

What is left of the cab as it stands today as a reminder of the Scammell's heritage.

The interior shows a different colour to the outside.

Pristine condition again! Awaiting the moment when the Gardner engine will burst into life.

An old-style fan belt is seen on the Scammell's pulleys. Take note of those cross ply tyres as used on the medium-tractor unit during its working career.

The winch assembly is shown here, without its cable. A winch such as this is an essential piece of tackle for any showman in the climate we live in. The chassis is gleaming in two-pack paint after blasting.

SHOWMAN ANCESTRY

PART TWO
Continued from last month.

Brian Timms concludes his own story about his fabulous 1942 showman's Scammell LA tractor.

By the summer of last year the cab was complete and had come back to Bodycraft for painting. Meanwhile the chassis had been blasted and painted, tyres put back on the wheels and the engine mounted in position. Autumn saw the truck back home with the cab fitted, standing in the garage especially constructed for it.

Ron Shrubb, a professional vintage wiring expert, sorted out the electrics once the instruments were back from Speedograph. The trusty 6LW was primed and fired up! This was done by Paul, Bodycraft's fitter, who was the first man to test run the vehicle. It all went without a hitch.

Now to fit the wings, a nerve-wracking task as they were in a extremely tight position, and being aluminium great care was required.

Trevor by now had finished the ballast box, with new timbers but using the original metal fittings. It was all too heavy to manhandle, so I called my good friend Robert Harris of the well-known showman's family Harris Bros of Ashington, Sussex. He arrived the next day with his ex-World War Two FWD/AEC Hiab rig. Placing the ballast box presented no further problems!

Finally the sign writer arrived, Mike 'Tommo' Thompson. He excelled himself with beautifully painted gallopers on the doors, namely 'Benny' and 'Irvin'. The doors were sign written 'Oliver Timms Amusements on Tour', after a grandson, and were resplendent in gold leaf. Irvin's gallopers motif on the front panel is a fine finishing touch.

The first public outing was at the Rudgwick Show in August, where it towed a turn of the century Orton & Spooner showman's living wagon built originally for Jimmy Wright, who travelled a shooting gallery between the wars.

Compelled by childhood experience and Thurston ancestry, the need to own a showman's rig has now been fulfilled!

Without doubt one of the most desirable Scammells in the country has come back to life, thanks to the efforts of Brian Timms and his team.

A fully refurbished and ready to go Gardner 6LW, the rebuilt 24 volt starter motor can be clearly seen.

A superb job of making a new cab was done by the team. Here Trevor Coldman takes time out to admire his workmanship.

Harris' come to the rescue with the FWD 'Special', as the well painted body is very carefully fitted in the later stages of the concours restoration.

The lifting straps were positioned so as to not touch the strong ballast box.

The metal has been neatly wrapped around the edge which gives it a quality touch.

The Gardner 6LW ticked over like a dream during our photographer's visit in August.

SOCIETY OF INDEPENDENT
MEMBER
ROUNDABOUT PROPRIETORS

The gold leaf sign writing has been done to a very high standard and is central on the panel, something that is not easy to do.

The living van's heritage is given away by the plate, as the van belonged to John Carter for a number of years. The Carters continue to travel their wonderful traditional fair.

Brian Timms, the man who resurrected the famous Irvin ex-London Metropolitan Water Board LA Scammell.

The outfit is ready to roll for its first rally in August 1999 down in deepest West Sussex.

The wings proved to be a problem, fitting the front ones more so than the rear.

The name 'Marvel' was used on the Irvin's 8hp Foster showman's engine 12499 which started life with William Irvin of Fleet, Hampshire. William said: "It's a marvel that he had been able to buy such a fine engine after so many ups and downs", and that's how the engine got its name. It's good to see the tradition carry on with internal combustion powered machinery.

As can be seen the winch fits snugly on top of the chassis frame, however, it needs a little more attention to get it to work correctly.

A considerable amount of time and money had to be spent sorting the headlights out.

The Orton & Spooner living van certainly looks the part in its purpose built awning.

Ton Up Scammell

by Mike Jeffries

The 100 ton Scammell was introduced to the public in November 1929 with two examples being built, KD 9168 and BLH 21. The latter example was new to HE Whey of Dartford, Kent, and in 1934 was acquired by Pickfords who used it until 1954. The other example KD 9168 was acquired by Marstons Road Services who were very much involved in the design of the vehicle.

In 1937 this example was acquired by Edward Box of Liverpool together with its special trailer, which was fitted with rails in different gauges for carrying locomotives. This outfit became famous for moving locomotives from the Vulcan works at Newton-le-Willows to Liverpool Docks for export all over the world.

The 100 tonners were originally fitted with Scammell's own four-cylinder, overhead valve seven-litre 86bhp petrol engine, this returned one mile to the gallon! It was not long before the 102bhp Gardner 6LW diesel unit was fitted. Eventually in 1949 KD 9168 joined its sister working for Pickfords. One tractor unit had higher gearing than the other. Gladly both examples have lasted into preservation. In our picture the unit is seen unloading a War Department 2-10-0 locomotive which is being shipped to Europe after D-Day in 1944.

All Mike's images are available in A3 or A4 format at £12.50 or £8.50 each. Tel: 01959 541400.

SCAMMELLS OF WATFORD

3600 gallon two-compartment general-purpose tanker. Tank shell insulated and fitted with heater coils. Loading by vacuum. Air pressure discharge.

3500 gallon fuel oil tanker. Scammell radial compressor on motive unit supplies air pressure for discharging load.

Motive unit for straight frame and other type semi-trailers showing twin headlamp equipment.

3275 gallon single-compartment bitumen tanker. Tank shell insulated and fitted with heater coils. Load discharge by air pressure.

3600 gallon single-compartment general purpose tanker with heat insulated tank shell. Vacuum loading. Discharge by air pressure from radial compressor on motive unit.

Overseas type motive unit with all-steel cab and roof canopy. Scammell radial compressor supplying air pressure for semi-trailer load discharge.

Motive unit and semi-trailers carrying cylinders for gas at pressures up to 3000 p.s.i. Heavy-duty automatic coupling

What a sight these Scammells make in all their colours and body styles. Classic and Vintage Commercials would be delighted to hear any reminiscences of driving these vehicles, or any other commercial vehicles come to that. See page 31 for posters advert. This poster is available from the Classic & Vintage Commercials store, tel: 01959 541444, Mon-Fri 9.00am-5.30pm.

Off the tracks
Part 1

David Reed pays tribute to some of the many preserved road vehicles with a rail connection seen at National Railway Museum events. In this first instalment, he looks back to earlier days and goes on to cover three-wheeled Scammell vehicles.

Road transport began to develop in the early years of the railways, with door-to-door collections and deliveries introduced in the 1840s. Since then, the two modes of transport have been linked in many ways.

Recognising this, the National Railway Museum in York has been holding a series of special Road and Railways events, with all manner of vehicles with a rail connection participating. Some are from the museum's collection, others privately owned.

Obviously the motive power at this time was horse power, with fleets expanding quickly as the railway network grew. Representing this period at one NRM event was Bristol based artist Ian Cryer with his 1899 GWR-built goods cart, fleet number 1720. It is thought that this

This horse ambulance dates from approximately 1900 and is the only one in existence. It can carry one or two horses - the back doors drop down and the floor slides out, with a cradle on board to support the horses. William supplies the motive power.

vehicle operated out of Bristol Temple Meads Station. It was restored by Ian in 1988. Pulled by the 12-year-old shire gelding 'Truman', it certainly added atmosphere to the gathering. Also seen was the Museum's horse ambulance dating from around 1900. It is the only one in existence and was used to rescue stricken animals. As well as providing the pulling power for deliveries, horses were used to shunt trucks in goods yards where the operation of a locomotive was deemed to be too expensive.

Trials of steam road vehicles by railway companies took place around 1900. The North Eastern Railway developed a Panhard engined parcels van at their Gateshead works in 1903, which later saw service in the York area, with more steam vehicles being authorised in 1904. Representing this period, but from a later date, was H Bell's 1928 Super Sentinel

Ian Cryer's 1899 goods wagon is a superb exhibit. It is seen here with 'Truman', a 12-year-old gelding.

Another vehicle from the Museum's collection, this Karrier Cob carries LMS colours.

steam wagon, which was new to George Senior & Son of Pond Street Forge, Sheffield, later passing to Pashley & Trickett of Rotherham. It was then operated by Brown Bayley's steel works in Sheffield and was last used in 1960. Restoration started in 1980 and included a new chassis and major fabrication work on the engine crankcase. It was first steamed after restoration in August 1986 with the project completed by April 1987.

With cheap war surplus vehicles available from the War Office, AECs and Leylands were used as well as American Peerless lorries which were being shipped into the UK.

Into the thirties, and a manoeuvrable form of transportation to rival the horse was becoming increasingly necessary, saving on fodder and vet bills. The answer was the Mechanical Horse. After early attempts built by Karrier, and the Napier Company who passed their project on to Scammells, development commenced. Chief Designer OD North's automatic

The NRM 1935 Motor Unit platform roller.

A 1953 Scammell Scarab on the weighbridge. Mike Manning of Scarborough is the owner.

coupling gear gave the vehicles the versatility required to pull a wide variety of trailers, along with the ability to turn in a 19ft circle with a 16ft trailer. The Scammell soon became a major success, and was represented at NRM events.

First there was a 1944 model, the origin of which is unknown. It was found in a scrapyard at Thrapston, Northants as a chassis with no engine or cab. It was rebuilt by Neville Grant and restored as an LNER vehicle. Neville has been associated with mechanical horses for many years. His father drove one, and he has a photograph of him sitting on his knee in the cab of one when he was four years old. Neville later worked on the vehicles at the Civil, Electrical and Mechanical Engineers Department at Croft Street, Ipswich. He says that the rules governing the descending of hills were that drivers had to

A smart Scammell six-tonner Mechanical Horse in GWR livery - this is another exhibit from the National Railway Museum.

get in a low gear, usually second, after stopping at the top of the hill. The reason was that it was thought that some drivers would not change down fast enough, having to stop, select a gear and put the trailer handbrake on as well as using the foot brake. Turning around on a hill was forbidden, and when they were parked up at night they had to be in 'echelon' order, that is the trailers parallel and straight with the cabs at an angle in order for a quick start the following day.

Another 'horse' was a 1934 model, bought in February of that year by the CME road motor department of the LNER at a cost of £177 13s 0d, excluding the trailer. It went into service at Ipswich as fleet vehicle HD 6518 on March 1 1934. In 1936 it was transferred to Bury St Edmunds North Depot. Authority for replacement was given in 1951 and on June 13 1952 the unit was de-licensed and withdrawn from service, having worked for 18 years and 4 months. It was sold to Peterborough Sports and Social Club in 1953 - the Scammell coupling was replaced with a draw bar and it was used to pull a set of gang mowers to cut the sports field grass. In April 1986 it was bought by Eric and Paddy Nunn at Emneth. It has been stripped down completely, the chassis shot blasted, engine overhauled, cab rebuilt, and a new front and a new petrol tank made. The coupling has also had to be remade, using borrowed original drawings and parts from other owners. It was eventually road worthy in April 1991 and is now one of the oldest units to survive.

Modernisation in the 1940s led to the Scarab, first produced in 1948. With around 12,000 being produced and 7,500 passing into railway service, they were seen throughout the country, epitomising the period. Seen at the NRM were a couple of examples of this well-known vehicle, including a 1957 model. This particular machine was delivered to Southend-on-Sea but was stored at Potters End Garage until 1962 when it was first registered. After withdrawal it was loaned to Beaulieu Motor Museum, but after some time went back to its then owner, National Carriers who sold it privately for preservation in 1990. During the NRM events, various vehicles had the chance to use the museum's weighbridge. The first vehicle to do so for 30 years was another Scarab, NDN 753 dating from 1953. It was based at Dewsbury and on retirement from the railways passed to dealers Matthewson of Thornton Dale in a poor state. It was bought by Mike Manning of Scarborough in 1996 and restored.

The final phase of three-wheeled Scammells was the Townsman, such as the 1966 example owned by John Downs from Keighley, West Yorks, EVY 477D. Like many of this type its working life was short, only operating until 1970 when it was sold for scrap. It was bought by John in 1984 for preservation.

Battery power had been experimented with for many years. The LMS were using battery power at their St Pancras goods depot as far back as 1917. During the '40s and '50s many battery powered units were put in service to be compared with the Scammells, including the Jensen Jen-Tug which had a lower capacity than the Scammell and due to its lightweight build had a shorter life span.

Other four-wheeled vehicles used included Karrier Bantams and later Bedford TK articulated tractors. Perhaps the rarest of the breed was the Scammell Scarab 4, of which only 150 were built. It carried a Standard Atlas front with the normal Townsman back. It was constructed by bolting the two halves of the chassis together, but proved an unsuccessful concept. Of those built, 140 were exported to South Africa. Where the 10 in the UK went is open to question, but if one could be found and preserved... ●

Coming soon:
Part 2. David Reed looks at four-wheeled vehicles with a rail connection.

This 1928 Super Sentinel steam wagon was last in commercial use in 1960, when working for Brown Bayley's steel works in Sheffield.

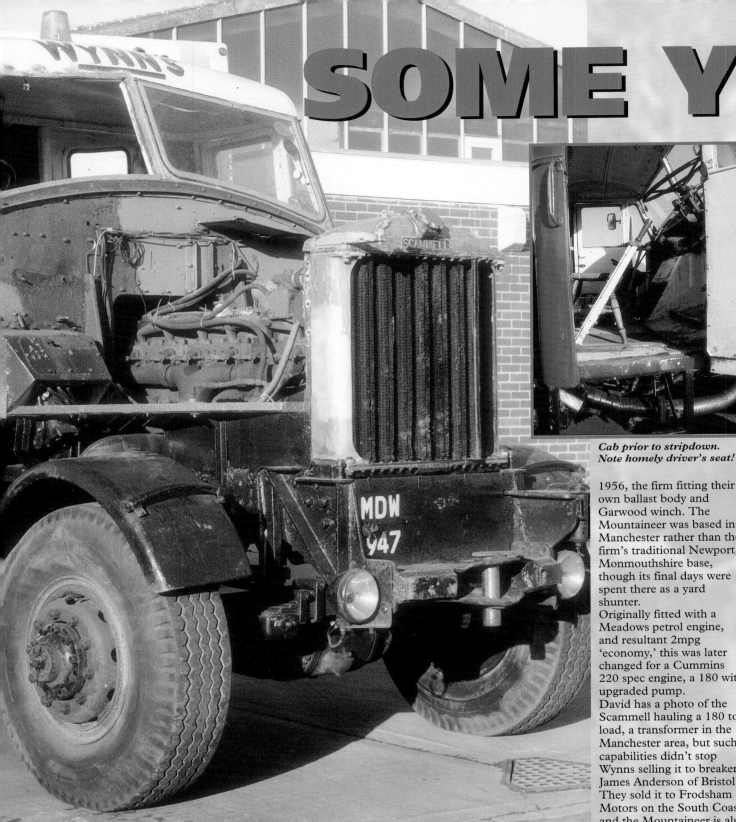

*Cab prior to stripdown.
Note homely driver's seat!*

Now here is something to look forward to! Restoration is cracking on with this fine Scammell Mountaineer ballast tractor, and the aim is to have it ready for the 2001 rally season.

When we tell you that behind the project is owner of nine classic trucks, Dave Gee of Gee's Haulage in Wakefield, Yorks, regular readers will know the standard the Scammell will be presented to the world.

David is a big Scammell fan, but that doesn't stop his collection including the superbly restored Volvo N10 featured in the March issue of *Classic and Vintage Commercials*, and a 1966 International Loadstar, assembled by International Harvester at Doncaster.

He has a slightly out of the ordinary approach to restoration: "I like to build a truck up to check for worn parts, and then strip it down again completely for repainting" he said.

Now for MDW 947's official history. It was new to Wynns, in chassis cab form in

1956, the firm fitting their own ballast body and Garwood winch. The Mountaineer was based in Manchester rather than the firm's traditional Newport, Monmouthshire base, though its final days were spent there as a yard shunter.

Originally fitted with a Meadows petrol engine, and resultant 2mpg 'economy,' this was later changed for a Cummins 220 spec engine, a 180 with upgraded pump.

David has a photo of the Scammell hauling a 180 ton load, a transformer in the Manchester area, but such capabilities didn't stop Wynns selling it to breakers James Anderson of Bristol. They sold it to Frodsham Motors on the South Coast, and the Mountaineer is also said to have spent a short time with Chipperfields Circus.

It also spent some time with Townsend Plant hire, who later sold the vehicle at auction. The Scammell then stood idle for some years before appearing in this magazine's classified pages. David made a successful bid, and the Mountaineer was triumphantly brought back to Wakefield.

A full stripdown of the body has taken place. New ash for the rebuild has been bought and a replacement bulkhead made.

The engine has been partly stripped, new oil seals being needed, and a new radiator is being built as you read this.

U WYNNS...

Restoration is forging ahead on this Scammell Mountaineer, said to be new to the legendary heavy haulage contractor, Wynns. But does it hold a secret?

Photos: Alec Kermotschuk

You wouldn't stand in its way, would you? Under restoration Scammell Moutaineer.

Imagine the bark from those exhausts!

"It's a 45-year-old vehicle and it's been standing for a long time and there's a lot of work to be done, probably a year's worth," said David, who does admit to getting diverted by his other projects, not least a 1956 Albion Chieftan, new to Smith's Crisps.

But David will scale the Mountaineer soon, though major jobs ahead include overhauling the relatively complex air brake system. "The Scammell will definitely have everything done on it. I always do everything that's needed," said David.

But he added that there was an unusual point about the vehicle. Stripping the paint off revealed the original grey, as was always the case, but then some green paint.

"This was never the case with Wynns, and I wonder if there's a secret to this vehicle's history."

As a Scammell Mountaineer doesn't match the Ford Escort in numbers there's obviously an easy solution to the question. Can anyone help?

Needless to say, we'll look forward to featuring this Scammell when restoration is complete. What a sight... and sound that will be!

Mighty Cummins 220 engine replaced original petrol Meadows unit!

SCAMMELLS SORTED!

We're back with the Hewitt family, whose superb Atkinson Borderer restoration featured in last month's issue. This time, their two contrasting but fine Scammells, a 1955 Constructor and 1976 Crusader are under the spotlight. Nick Larkin reports.

Main photos: Garry Stuart.

Crusader painted to depict a Wynns vehicle - a period sun visor is still needed!

Family loyalties can be complex! The Hewitts, as very much confirmed in last month's story of their fine Borderer restoration, are dyed-in-the-wool Atkinson fans but well, they've always had a thing about Scammells, too.

Peter Hewitt originally comes from the Isle of Wight, his brother and sister still live there and there are many other family connections with the Island.

On one such trip an unexpected discovery was made. "I'd gone to see a chap who used to help my dad out and was reading his copy of *Classic and Vintage Commercials* when I saw that someone locally wanted a 6LW Gardner engine for a 1943 Scammell, I had friends with one so I rang the chap up and went to see him early Sunday morning. He had an ex-Shell/BP tractor unit.

"We got talking, and I said I'd been originally after a Mountaineer, which is the four-wheel version of the Constructor. He said he knew where there was one, so we got in my car and went to Newport and down by the quay in a place they call Little London were the gravel works." A wonderful, if tatty sight greeted Peter; a 1955 Constructor.

"She hadn't moved for two years. I looked around her and she didn't look too bad."

The Scammell's owner wanted to sell, and so Peter and son Michael made a further visit.

"We gave the Constructor a thorough examination, and made sure the winch and all the various ratios worked." recalls Peter.

Peter agreed he'd have the Scammell but under one condition, saying to the owner: "You're not having the money until I get to the boat. It's got to drive the six miles to East Cowes." It was taxed as a crane, meaning no MoT was necessary for the journey.

The deal was agreed, and not surprisingly dock and ferry staff and passengers were somewhat shocked when the Scammell, which to them must have looked like a vehicle from Mad Max, rolled up ready for transport back to the mainland. The family's Atkinson and low loader were waiting on the other side of the Solent ready to take the Scammell back to Warwickshire.

Once back home, a programme of major work began on the vehicle, one of around 80 examples built for the Army.

Not a lot is known about the Scammell's subsequent history, though it is rumoured to have spent some time in Preston. It had, though, been on the Isle of Wight for a long time, when it was used as a winching tractor for a stone company on the River Medina.

A Leyland 600 engine had been fitted in place of the original Meadows petrol unit, and this gives the 15 ton Scammell 7-8mpg, as opposed the original 2-3. Not surprisingly the engine is to be retained,

Fifteen tons of fun - the Scammell Constructor.

Access to Crusader's engine by lifting out hinged radiator.

Winch will operate sideways, forwards and backwards.

Left-hand drive Crusader's cab.

though the Euclid colour the unit is painted in suggests it was originally used in plant.

Much work has been done so far, including a conversion of the handbrake from ratchet to modern spring break. The head gasket has been changed, as have all the oils.

"The brakes had come to the stage where they were just about non-existent, someone had adjusted the brakes on the rods so all the fulcrums were too far forward. I've stripped the system down and adjusted brakes and hubs and set all the linkage up as the brake pedal went right to the floor," said Peter.

A new control box is to be fitted as part of an electrical overhaul.

Bodywork attention is also high on the agenda. "Ideally, the cab wants to come off, though it's difficult to do this where the Scammell is stored, so we'll probably do the work in sections," said Peter. Just for the record, if the Scammell's screen arrangement looks strangely familiar don't be surprised. It's the same as that fitted to a Bedford O-series.

The winch fitted to the vehicle is the type normally associated with the Pioneer, and the ballast weight is also from an earlier Scammell. The winch should have ⅞in cable, but an inch cable had been fitted, and this situation is to be rectified.

A good look over the Hewitt's Constructor would convince anyone that this vehicle is a prime example of precision heavy engineering, for example the front axle, with its massive differential is designed to work efficiently on only one gallon of EP90 oil.

There's a 12-speed high/low ratio gearbox with transfer box, from which two shafts drive the front and rear axle respectively.

Air-assisted power steering has been fitted from new. Then there's a hand throttle and a hill brake, even a rev counter remaining from the days when the Scammell had a petrol engine.

To operate the winch, the transfer box is locked in neutral, you put your power take-off in, select gear you want to pull out, a dog clutch engages top of winch and you're away!

The Constructor as found on the Isle of Wight.

Constructor's winch believed to be from Pioneer. A ⅞in rather than the present inch thick cable should be fitted.

Leyland 600 engine has replaced original petrol Meadows unit.

Constructor's instruments; note rev counter from petrol engined days; the device with a small chain attached fits over the headlight switch as a reminder of secretive night time manoeuvres.

What an incredible machine!

The second Scammell is more sophisticated, but still beautifully engineered. It's a January 1976 Crusader heavy haulage tractor, complete with left-hand drive as it was built for the army in Germany, being registered 23 GJ 76.

It was spotted for sale at Meadows Plant in Bracknell, Berkshire. Michael Hewitt takes up the story. "He had three or four of them, and used them to move tanks for Bovington tank museum, but they were eventually offered for sale."

The Scammell had also been used to move tanks for the army, and latterly as a training vehicle.

Since entering the Hewitts' fleet the Scammell had been in regular use. Most work needed was to the cab.

"Crusader cabs were all built by Motor Panels cabs of Coventry and were terrible for rot," said Michael. "This vehicle wasn't too bad, the main rot was on the panels, though a lot of plating and filling to the floor near the driver's side was also needed. The door skins were plated, as obviously the Hewitts didn't want to have to buy new doors.

Added Michael: "Shotblasting was horrendous as the army must have painted it more than washed it. There were layers and layers of paint but every nut and bolt on it was galvanised, which meant they weren't seized up."

The cab does have much in its favour though: "You can sleep in the Scammell as it's a double bunk and the cabs were built and insulated for anywhere in the world, so it's a fantastically warm cab and good to sleep in.

"The 305 Rolls-Royce engine, an

Cab needs attention, and ideally should be removed for repair.

uprated 290, has only needed a good service. The Crusader has a 15-speed Fuller gearbox with splitter. The Atkinson was nearly finished when we bought the Scammell. We drove it home and all it needed was bodywork."

A set of new tyres was fitted and the Scammell was ready for action. But then came the cosmetic problem of paint. Michael again: "We didn't want to leave it in army colours as all your oily fingerprints showed up. A lot of shows put army vehicles in one corner and we wanted to display the Crusader and the Atkinson

The Constructor heads for the mainland from Isle of Wight ferry.

Crusader cabs are notorious for rot, and the Hewitts' vehicle was no exception.

Crusader as bought in Army guise.

together, so what do you do? Put it in a fictitious colour with your own name on it or do you find a company running a similar vehicle and put it in their colour scheme?"

The result is a vehicle presented in Wynns' livery. "What gave us the idea of doing it was that Seddon Atkinson had got a W&J Ridings Atkinson Mk 1 which wasn't ex-Riding but new to Suttons of St Helens. I believe Suttons had gone on to foreign vehicles and they didn't want to put it in Suttons colours," Michael recalled.

"That gave me an idea. A friend put me in touch with John Wynn and he said 'Yes, put in my colours by all means,' but he was very particular on which vehicle he wanted. He wanted to get a feel for the sort of job we'd do. I sent him pictures of the Atkinson and he said 'yes, great.' He was very, very helpful."

As with the Atkinson, paintwork was carried out by a friend of the family, Stuart Davis, at his Stoke Golding workshop.

An original Wynn's sun visor is now sought to complete the effect. "All of Wynns vehicles had them, When we put the sun visor on we can fit the proper Wynns headboard," said Michael.

The vehicle's brakes were good, with only a hub seal having to be replaced. A hub seal on the diff pinion and some work on the springs comprised the rest of the necessary mechanical work

Like the Atkinson, the Crusader has been restored with regular use in mind, often to assist the preservation movement.

"We use it as a winching tractor, it will winch sideways, forwards and backwards," Michael revealed.

"The biggest day's work it did was at Banbury Show two or three years ago and everything was sinking in the mud. We went up there the night before to have a nice leisurely drink with some of the Scammell and Atki owners, but ended up winching vehicles out of the mire for three or four hours - including the ERF B-series owned by Dave Cole with a traction engine on back of low loader which we had to winch it across 2 fields. He'd gone 3-4 days earlier when it was dry couldn't get off the site. Undulations on the field meant the unit kept bottoming out."

Both vehicles make regular rally appearances, the Hewitts particularly enjoying the Crick event. The Atkinson usually trailers the Scammell to shows.

How do the family sum up their Scammells? "The Constructor is the ultimate piece of engineering and the Crusader's another world, with a lot of room in the well insulated cab.... and it's a good winching tractor!" ●

The Hewitt family, from left, Sean, an hgv mechanic, wife Sarah, Peter, Michael and son James and Michael's wife Amanda.

MAKING ALL THE RIGHT MOVES

Moving house can often literally mean moving your house in some parts of the world. Pat Ware finds out more, and reports on an historic recent move involving a regularly used 60-year-old British Scammell.

An extraordinary 'Millennium move.' Watkins' 1941 Scammell Pioneer gun tractor is still in regular use moving houses - literally.

Although the soaring property prices we've seen in some parts of the country are beginning to settle down again, newspapers still seem to be full of advice about 'moving house.'

On the other side of the globe this seemingly innocent phrase can often be taken literally.

In Australia and New Zealand,ˇ it is not at all unusual to shift a house, either to a completely new plot of land or simply a few yards to make way, for example, for a road widening scheme.

With a little bit of excavation, or, for example, by shifting the 'sleeper' walls, the whole house can be jacked up on its bottom bearers, mostly in one piece. This allows a purpose-designed trailer, which is often telescopic to accommodate buildings of all shapes and sizes, to be slid underneath.

It only takes about an hour, using a series of eightˇ ton hydraulic jacks, to lift a typical building by one metre, sufficient for loading.

Aside from the obvious difficulties of actually lifting and moving the house without damage, part of the skill lies in calculating the weight of the building. Obviously, there's no way it can be weighed while still on the ground, so rules of thumb and experience are the order of the day - apparently a typical timber-framed building weighs between one and two tons per 10 square metres of floor area, but much depends on the density of the timber used in its construction.

Calculating the weight was not always the exact science it has become today, and in the past it seems the hauliers used to get away with murder. In the 1950 and 60s it seems no-one outside the industry really had any idea of the weight of a house. The traffic police would take the word of the haulage company, who would often divide the real weight by a factor of two or three.

Massive houses were shifted on trailers with just two or three axles, and bridge weight restrictions were blissfully exceeded.

Then the authorities started to use axle scales. For a while, the hauliers managed to convince them that the scales were wrong, but eventually the game was up, and it became apparent that the '15 ton' houses everyone had been blithely dragging around the country in fact weighed closer to 30 or more tons.

Now, of course, the authorities are very much concerned with the environmental damage caused by excess axle loadings, and everyone is a little more circumspect.

Once the house has been lifted and the weight (correctly!) calculated, it can be loaded on to the trailer. Then, theoretically, it's just a matter of towing the whole thing along the public highway to a new location.

House hauliers Watkins used this Guy FBAX in the 1950s. The vehicle had a telescopic trailer, seen here with a nautical load.

However, the actual move has to be planned down to the last detail, with overhead and power lines and road signs often having to be lifted or moved, and the widths and heights of bridge parapets carefully checked for clearance.

Needless to say, this requires a fair degree of co-operation from the police and local authorities - you certainly wouldn't want to let a 60ft house loose on the roads in the rush hour!

House moving is a fascinating and unusual task which is undertaken by a particular breed of heavy haulage men who specialise in this type of work, often moving relatively large buildings. One such haulier is Kevin Watkins, of Hastings, New Zealand. He's the owner of Watkins Building Movers, a third generation family haulage business where, alongside more conventional tasks, like both his father and grandfather before him Ken specialises in house moves.

As long ago as 1914, Kevin's grandfather, Alf, was using a McClaren steam traction engine to move buildings. In one documented move, a two storey building was split in half vertically, and used as two loads. Whilst the split simplified the move, the New Zealand roads were not felt to be adequate for the weight, and the road had to be planked for the entire route to prevent the wooden wheeled trailer from breaking through the surface.

By the late 1940s, Kevin's father, Vic Watkins, was using a couple of war surplus trucks - a forward control Guy FBAX 6x4 three-ton searchlight chassis, and a 1941 Scammell Pioneer R100 artillery tractor.

When Kevin inherited the business, he acquired a second Pioneer, and still uses it to this day. That's right, he uses a 60-year-old ex-military truck in pursuit of his everyday business.

The Scammell was first used by the British Army in World War 2, and then saw action in Korea, before being sold to the New Zealand Army and remaining in service until 1973.

By the time the Watkins bought it, the old Pioneer was, as Ken says, "well used," but although the truck was 300 miles from their home base they simply put in a new battery, pumped up the tyres and drove her home, at a maximum 24 mph!

The Pioneer may lack some of the creature comforts of more modern trucks, but when the going gets tough the military heritage starts to assert itself! While the big boys in their 500bhp rigs might smirk when they pass the trusty Scammell on the highway, as Kevin says: "The smile can soon be wiped off their faces when they get into trouble in the sticky stuff and the Scammell is called upon to pull them out."

At just 10 minutes past midnight, with the job successfully completed, haulier Kevin Watkins and wife Denise enjoy a well-earned glass of bubbly.

53

The Watkins' Scammell was originally a gun tractor, Here's how it would have looked during military service.

The Pioneer may be cold and draughty on a winter morning and can be tiring on the bendy bits of road, but as Kevin says, once you understand the funny little ways of the Scammell six-speed gearbox: "She's a darling to drive, and gives every indication she'll go on forever."

Replacement parts could be a problem, but these days the truck only covers about 4000 miles a year. The firm still owns the original Pioneer acquired back in the 1940s which can be used as a parts donor if necessary.

The Pioneer is still powered by Gardner's superb 6LW diesel, exactly as the truck was when it left Tolpits Lane, Watford, so long ago. Gardner parts are still generally available, but fortunately are seldom required. A recent New Zealand TV programme on diesel engines claims the Gardner 6LW was the finest diesel ever made, and Kevin says "amen to that."

Knowing of my fondness for ancient Scammells, Kevin recently wrote and told me of a well-planned operation in which he and his trusty Pioneer made heavy vehicle history by moving the first house of the new Millennium.

The house in question was owned by the Hill family, and the move, which was actually of less than 500 yards distance, was necessitated by the splitting up of a large agricultural estate in order to share it between a number of sons.

All were sworn to secrecy, until, at one minute past midnight on January 1 2000, the New Zealand night air resounded to the smooth sound of the Gardner 6LW as the near 60-year-old Scammell Pioneer gun tractor took up the strain, moving on on to the public highway with a full-size bungalow, weighing about 18 tonnes, in tow.

Within ten minutes the exciting part was over and the load was parked alongside the new site ready to be settled on to its new foundations the next morning.

The Hill family, delighted at their part in making world house moving history, provided a great feast of edibles and a couple of bottles of best Antipodean bubbly. Kevin, and his wife Denise, enjoyed a well-earned tipple by the side of the road with the house and trailer forming a backdrop.

Kevin says the Millennium Move was: "a fantastic chance to honour a fantastic vehicle."

There must be millions of heavy trucks worldwide, but only one can claim to have moved the first oversized load of the 21st century... and that truck 'just happened' to be a 60-year-old Scammell.

Let me close with a word of warning. Out in the former colonies, houses are generally built with a timber frame and a structure generally more flexible than our brick built homes. So don't try this one at

A house move in earlier days, this dwelling being removed from a hilltop, again using the FBAX. The situation isn't as precarious as it looks, as the 40 foot side house was connected to a heavy bulldozer to prevent it 'running away.'

SCAMMELL

At Work

Originally founded in 1837, the Scammell company started truck manufacture in 1920, exhibiting an innovative six-wheeled articulated chassis at Olympia. Scammell claimed the vehicle provided a '7½-ton payload with 3-ton operating costs', and its success led to the creation of Scammell Lorries Limited.

Heavy trucks soon became a speciality, and Scammell was the first to produce a genuine '100-tonner'. The articulated tractor remained in production almost throughout the life of the company, and

with the powerful Pioneer, and the so-called Rigid 8, the company continued to prosper through the Second World War... but hard times lay ahead, and in 1955, Scammell was taken over by Leyland.

Under Leyland ownership, some of the companyís best-known models were produced - the Highwayman, Handyman, Routeman, Explorer and Constructor - as well as the lesser-known Himalayan, Sherpa and Mountaineer. During the Seventies and Eighties, the model range included the Crusader and the massive Contractors and Commanders. And, of course, for over 30 years, Scammell produced the three-wheeled Mechanical Horse and its successors, the Scarab and Townsman.

In 1987, DAF took over the Leyland Trucks Division, and within 12 months, Scammell's famous Watford factory was closed and the name consigned to history. The rights to manufacture the Scammell models were acquired by Unipower, albeit under its own name, and Unipower continues to provide logistic support for many Scammell models, as well as manufacturing specialised heavy vehicles.

Pat Ware is a keen commercial-vehicle enthusiast, military-vehicle historian and author, contributing regularly to Classic and Vintage Commercials. A particular fan of all things Scammell, he has written and published four titles devoted to the company's military vehicles.

In 1920, G Scammell & Nephew demonstrated an articulated six-wheeled tractor-lorry to the trade press, later launching it to the public at the 1921 Olympia Motor Show. Designed to exploit the law governing tractors and trailers, this articulated chassis and trailer was considered to be a single unit, meaning it could legally carry a 7½-ton payload, at a dizzying maximum speed of 12mph. (Watford Museum)

Scammell's 'six-wheeled tractor-lorry' was hugely successful, and it was not long before a new company, Scammell Lorries Ltd., was established. In 1922, the operation moved from London's Fashion Street to a new factory at Tolpits Lane, Watford, where it remained until 1988. This typical tractor unit, by now with a hard-topped cab and fixed-screen, was probably produced in 1922. The photograph clearly shows the chain-drive rear axle and large-diameter turntable ('fifth wheel' as we would now call it).

The early success of the company helped to fuel technical developments, and in June 1927, Scammell announced the Pioneer, a heavy tractor intended for oil-field and military use. Designed by the talented Oliver North, who remained with the company from 1923 until retirement in 1948, the 6x4 and 6x6 Pioneer used innovative walking-beam gear-cases, combined with a pivoting front axle and huge balloon tyres, to provide literally wall-climbing performance. (Watford Museum)

Scammell was not exclusively a constructor of heavy trucks and, for more than 30 years, produced the unique Mechanical Horse with its front-mounted engine placed over the single wheel. Although the concept was conceived of by Napier, Scammell bought it in 1931 and, under the hand of Oliver North, evolved into a three-wheeled tractor-trailer combination much loved by railway parcel services and municipal authorities. This 1933 example has a refuse collection body. (National Motor Museum)

Not all haulage companies were comfortable with the tractor-and-trailer combination, and in 1936, Scammell announced the Rigid 8, a four-axle truck which could carry a payload of 15 tons within a 22-ton gross vehicle weight (GVW). Renamed Routeman in 1960, and subsequently metamorphosing into the S26 in 1980 with an uprated GVW of 30-tons, the basic four-axle design remained in production throughout the life of the company. This tanker-bodied example, intended for carrying sugar products, dates from around 1958.

Of course, the archetypal military Scammell was the 6x4 Pioneer that saw service as a gun tractor, tank transporter and recovery vehicle throughout WW2. This R100 gun tractor, one of 980 manufactured between 1935 and 1942, was photographed in 1937 towing a 60-pounder gun belonging to 'Number 4 battery, Royal Artillery'. The Pioneer was offered with a choice of Scammell's own 7-litre petrol engine or the incomparable Gardner 6LW diesel - the Gardner was specified for all the military versions.

By the end of the decade, Pioneers been supplied to Venezuela, Iraq and India. This chassis, photographed in 1931, in front of the 'famous' Tolpits Lane allotments, was subsequently fitted with a cargo body and, to great critical acclaim, was demonstrated to representatives of the British Australian Gold Mining Company and to the trade press. Note the huge vertical-spindle winch. (National Motor Museum)

In 1938, Scammell produced this distinctive 4x4 winching tractor for the Admiralty. Front-wheel-drive was provided by a modified version of the standard epicyclic unit used at the rear, with a single-speed transfer case providing power to the axles. This is probably the only example that was constructed and, like many Scammells, saw out its working life on the fairground.

The Pioneer recovery tractor (SV/1S and SV/2S) remained in service with the British Army until the 1970s. Posed, as with so many Scammell official photographs, in front of the allotments, this 1939-built SV/1S tractor shows off its hand-operated folding jib and wooden-panelled body. More than 2000 examples of the recovery tractor were supplied between 1936 and 1945. (British Commercial Vehicle Museum Trust)

The Pioneer tank-transporter variant was originally rated at 20 tons, but it soon became obvious that this was insufficient and it was upgraded to 30 tons - even this proving inadequate for the larger tanks of WW2. The 30-ton version (TRMU30) employed two types of semi-trailer. This Scammell photograph, from 1940, shows the early trailer with a continuous slope to the load bed. (British Commercial Vehicle Museum Trust)

For carrying bulk fluids and powders, in 1924, Scammell developed the 'frameless tanker' concept - the rear bogie and turntable were attached directly to the tank to provide an increase of some 15cwt in useful payload. Motive power was provided by a bonneted tractor unit, a direct descendent of the original six-wheeled tractor-lorry, using a Gardner diesel or Scammell-Meadows petrol engine. Although it is often described as the Highwayman, the name was not actually adopted until after the 1955 Leyland takeover. This example, dating from 1944, carries the first such tank with an elliptical shape, and is loaded with civilian wartime 'pool petrol'.

Based on the chassis of the 20-ton drawbar tractor, the Showtrac was designed specifically for travelling fairground operators. The coach-built ballast body housed a 450A generator and 10-ton mechanical winch, and the engine, normally a Gardner 6LW, provided sufficient power to allow the vehicle to haul two or three trailers at respectable road speeds. This example, one of 18 constructed between 1945 and 1948, was delivered new in 1946 to Frank Harniess, passing to Wigfields in the Sixties.

By the end of the War, the Pioneer was clearly past its prime and the War Office planned its replacement with more modern machinery from Leyland and Thornycroft. However, in 1950, when deliveries of the recovery variant were not coming through quickly enough, Scammell came up with the 6x6 Explorer as an interim measure. The Gardner diesel of the Pioneer was unaccountably replaced by a Scammell-Meadows petrol engine, and the vehicle offered all-wheel-drive, but the Explorer drew very heavily on the Pioneer design philosophy. It was included in the Scammell catalogue for many years, but the Explorer was not favoured by commercial operators. (National Motor Museum)

Although it used a more conventional rear bogie configuration, the 6x6 Constructor was also in the Pioneer mould. The chassis was offered as a fifth-wheel tractor for use with a semi-trailer, as a rigid oil-field tractor, and steel-bodied ballast tractor. This example was used by the Royal Engineers for moving heavy plant; note the Pioneer-like front mudguards. In production from 1952 until 1983, the Constructor was a very capable vehicle favoured by both military and commercial operators, particularly overseas - of the 1257 Contractors produced, less than 100 were sold on the home market. The usual power unit was a Rolls-Royce C6 diesel, but Cumminsí units were also available. (British Commercial Vehicle Museum Trust)

This airbrush illustration clearly demonstrates the indignities to which the Explorer (or Pioneer) chassis could be subjected while keeping its wheels in contact with the ground. The walking-beam gearcases at the rear allow the wheels on either side to move relative to one another by up to a foot in the vertical plane; while at the front, the A-frame design allows the axle to pivot by two-feet from bump to rebound. (British Commercial Vehicle Museum Trust)

Motive unit and semi-trailers carrying cylinders for gas at pressures up to 3000 p.s.i. Heavy-duty automatic coupling

3600 gallon single-compartment general purpose tanker with heat insulated tank shell. Vacuum loading. Discharge by air pressure from radial compressor on motive unit.

3600 gallon two-compartment general-purpose tanker. Tank shell insulated and fitted with heater coils. Loading by vacuum. Air pressure discharge.

The Highwayman was arguably Scammell's most popular tractor unit and was available with a huge array of user-specified options allowing the customer to literally 'mix-and-match' to suit the particular job. As the brochure said: *'Scammell Lorries Limited offers a unique service - designing and supplying vehicles to suit individual requirements and providing the most efficient and economical solution to road transport problems.'*

Overseas type motive unit with all-steel cab and roof canopy. Scammell radial compressor supplying air pressure for semi-trailer load discharge.

3500 gallon fuel oil tanker. Scammell radial compressor on motive unit supplies air pressure for discharging load.

Motive unit for straight frame and other type semi-trailers showing twin headlamp equipment.

3275 gallon single-compartment bitumen tanker. Tank shell insulated and fitted with heater coils. Load discharge by air pressure.

2700 gallon single-compartment rubber-lined hydrochloric acid tanker. Heavy-duty automatic coupling.

2370 gallon single-compartment glucose tanker. Tank shell heat insulated. Load discharge by power-driven pump on motive unit.

Articulated 8-wheeled transporter for abnormal and indivisible loads. Payload capacities up to 30 tons.

495 cu. ft. capacity bulk cement tanker. Using compressor on motive unit load can be discharged up to 100 ft. vertically or 1000 ft. horizontally at the rate of 1 ton per minute.

4 × 2 tractor for drawbar trailers. Suitable for gross train weights up to 52 tons.

1620 gallon single-compartment rubber-lined sulphuric acid tanker. Load discharge by air pressure from radial compressor on motive unit.

4000 gallon stepped elliptical stainless steel chemical tanker. Outlets from five compartments manifolded to central discharge point. Heavy-duty automatic coupling

The War Office also bought a number of fifth-wheel Constructors, including a handful for use by the RAF. On this variant, the cab is more like the standard design used on the Explorer and the early Highwayman, rather than the Bedford-derived unit fitted to most Constructors. Posing during a break in testing at the Fighting Vehicles Research and Development Establishment (FVRDE), this particular vehicle has survived into preservation. (British Commercial Vehicle Museum Trust)

This pair of Constructor ballast tractors was supplied to the Singapore Public Utilities Board in 1964. Designed for use with a purpose-made 10-axle 150-ton Fruehauf low-bed trailer, they were intended for moving heavy electrical plant from the docks to a power-station scheme. The pressed-steel wheels and road tyres clearly say civilian, but otherwise, these vehicles are little different from the military ballast tractors introduced more than a decade earlier.

Directly descended from the original six-wheeled tractor-lorry concept, Scammell's most popular tractor unit was the bonneted 4x2, dubbed Highwayman from 1955. After Leyland's takeover, the vehicle usually sported an O.600 or O.680 engine, but earlier examples generally used a Gardner. The Highwayman remained in production until 1970. This 1959 example features the glassfibre cab and wrap-around windscreen introduced alongside the standard coach-built and pressed-steel units towards the end of the production run. Note the separate cycle wings, a feature particularly favoured by Pickfords. The driver and his mate struggle with a Planet industrial diesel locomotive on the low-loader trailer.

Another 1959 Highwayman, this time a frameless tanker belonging to Shell-Mex BP and finished in the smart red-and-green corporate livery of the period. The large, square front wings were the standard offering. The photograph was taken in Northern Ireland and reflects an altogether more peaceful period in the history of the province.

Although the Mountaineer, Sherpa and Himalayan model ranges included purpose-designed dump trucks, Scammell was essentially a custom truck builder and customers often asked for a one-off. This is a 6x4 Junior Constructor, a design usually favoured by Pickfords and Wynns as a ballast tractor, fitted with a large scow-ended dumper body. Powered by the Leyland O.680 engine, the Junior Constructor was introduced in 1957 and also differed from its larger parent in having a non-driven front axle.

Not all Highwayman chassis were used as tractor units - this unusual five-cubic-yard dumper dates from the late Fifties and was built on the standard tractor chassis with its short 10-foot wheelbase. Compare the traditional coach-built cab with its flat windscreen to the more-modern appearance of the glassfibre unit.

The old Rigid 8 changed its name to Routeman in 1960 but the four-axle design remained one of the company's longest-lived models - this example dates from the first year of Routeman production. Power was provided by either a Gardner or Leyland unit. The rather clumsily-styled glassfibre cab was shared with the contemporary forward-control Handyman tractor and was clearly derived from the Highwayman unit, but it has not been improved by the styling changes necessary to accommodate the forward-control layout.

Following the introduction of the Junior Constructor in 1957, the Constructor range was widened again in 1958 by the Super Constructor, a powerful 6x6 tractor powered by either a Leyland O.900 or supercharged Rolls-Royce C6S, and with eight-speed semi-automatic transmission. Although a handful appeared in Pickfords' and Sunters' liveries with impressive crew cabs, the Super Constructor was a favourite for overseas heavy-haulage duties. This example, coupled to a curious double-pivot six-axle trailer, was delivered to Quarry Industries of New South Wales in 1964. Note the mechanical hand-signal device on the driver's door!

The original Mechanical Horse remained in production until 1948 when it was superseded by the Scarab, in turn replaced by the Townsman in 1964. Like its predecessor, the Scarab was available in three- and six-ton versions, and although the engine was moved to behind the cab, the basic concept remained unchanged. Power was generally provided by a Scammell petrol engine, but some used a Perkins diesel. Seen here, in service with the Midlands Region of British Railways, is a Scarab 6 tractor and semi-trailer combination dating from around 1950. (National Motor Museum)

Along with the similar 4x2 Sherpa, the half-cab 6x4 Himalayan was a result of Scammell's foray into producing purpose-designed dump trucks. It was introduced in 1961 and remained in production for more than a decade, but with just 75 produced, it was scarcely a runaway success. Fitted with a Leyland O.680 diesel, the vehicle had a payload rating of 12/14 cubic yards and was intended only for off-road use.

The four-axle Routeman was given a face-lift in 1962 when it was fitted with the striking Michelotti-designed glassfibre cab. Dubbed the Routeman 2, this in turn was replaced by the similar Routeman 3 in 1969. Photographed in 1971, Scammell's demonstrator wears a light-alloy twin-hoist tipper body, finished in the group livery. The Routeman remained in production until 1980 and was available with a choice of Gardner, Leyland and Rolls-Royce Eagle power units.

In late 1960, Scammell announced the forward-control 6x4 Trunker. This was designed to exploit impending changes to 'construction and use' regulations, which were to allow articulated vehicles to be enlarged to a 32-ton GVW. The vehicle featured a rear-mounted Gardner 6HLX engine and double-drive Albion bogie, combined with an innovative air-suspended four-wheeled semi-trailer. The cab was the standard Leyland-Albion-Dodge (LAD) design widely used within the Leyland group. Unfortunately, handling problems meant that only three examples were constructed before the model was quietly dropped.

Visually, the Routeman 3 differed very little from its predecessor, the most noticeable difference being the use of rectangular headlamps introduced to coincide with an increase in GVW to 30 tons in 1972. At the same time, the driveline was standardised as 8x4, where previous examples had also been available with an 8x2 configuration. This Leyland-powered bulk-refuse vehicle, dating from 1979, carries Lacre bodywork.

Scammells were always popular in the heavy-haulage sector, and in 1964, the massive Contractor was introduced for this market. From small beginnings, the range expanded to include seven basic chassis types suitable for a maximum (conservatively-rated) 240-ton gross train weight. The trucks were always built to order and there was a long list of options covering chassis, cab, power train and driveline configuration; for example, the buyer could choose Rolls-Royce, AEC, Leyland or Cummins engines, driving through a Leyland, Self Changing Gears or Fuller gearbox. This example is a relatively-modest fifth-wheel tractor dating from the first year of production and destined for South Africa.

The Trunker 1 had been a commercial failure and although it was re-launched as the Trunker 2 in 1965, Scammell almost immediately started work on a replacement. Named the Crusader, the new tractor was launched at the 1968 Commercial Motor Show and was powered by a choice of Leyland, GM, Rolls-Royce and AEC engines. It was also available with either a 6x2 or 6x4 driveline, the latter being mostly for export. Most Crusaders were specified as tractor units, but the British Army bought a number equipped with EKA recovery gear. This 4x2 tractor was caught on trade plates on a very wet motorway.

ICI purchased a number of these Contractors with special side-tipping Dyson trailers for use at a Derbyshire quarry. With a GVW of 85 tons, the bodies carried up to 50 tons of limestone. Power was provided by a Rolls-Royce 305 diesel driving through an RV30 eight-speed semi-automatic gearbox. Although scarcely recognisable, the cab is the standard LAD design also employed on the Trunker, albeit now with a formidable bonnet.

The MoD also toyed with the S24, an impressive bonneted tractor that had replaced the Contractor in 1980. Available in both 6x4 and 6x6 configurations, the S24 shared cab and general chassis arrangements with the Scammell-designed Leyland Landtrain, and was the company's last commercial heavy-haulage tractor. Like the Contractor, it was available with either a ballast body or fifth-wheel coupling, and with a wide range of options. This 6x6 example, tested by the MoD, was Cummins-powered.

After WW2, the Pioneer tank transporters were replaced by Thornycroft Mighty Antars, but by 1968, it was obvious that these were past their prime and Scammell started the design work which eventually led to the Commander. During one of the periodic project cancellations, the Ministry of Defence (MoD) briefly considered off-the-shelf tank transporters and Scammell proposed the forward-control S26. Introduced in the early 1980s to replace the Crusader, the Cummins-powered S26 was more normally badged a Leyland, but it had already been sold to a number of armies and was more than capable of hauling the requisite 65 tons. Despite trials, the MoD did not buy.

WE LOVE LA!

We've been featuring regularly the ongoing restoration of renowned Yorkshire restorer and haulier, Dave Gee's ex-Wynns Scammell Mountaineer, but until now have neglected his other fine example of the marque, a 1937 LA.

Photos: Alec Kermotschuk

Scammell in its eye-catching, immaculate blue and Post Office red.

Dave Gee is a Scammell fanatic – our features on the chassis-up rebuild of his fine ex-Wynns Mountaineer prove this without doubt. Fingers crossed, we'll see this major project completed by the end of this year.

His collection also includes a Volvo N10, the restoration of which was featured in our March 2000 issue, and an equally well-known 1966 International Harvester Loadstar.

But Dave has a second Scammell, now immaculately presented, which has seen less of the limelight but which has some significant gaps in its fascinating history.

A 1937 LA tractor, a model which continued into the war, this Scammell is believed to have been new to Esso Petroleum, possibly as a tanker (more on this further on). The LA now carries the registration FSU 404, which we presume was issued in recent years from unused DVLA pre-suffix stocks.

By the end of its days, the LA had been relegated to use as a shunter at Esso's Fawley, Southampton, refinery before finally being sold at an auction.

Previous owner John Bilkey, of St Stephen, Cornwall, carried out an initial restoration. This work included reinstating the original four-piece windscreen – the windscreen had been modified by Esso

into a two-piece unit.

Eventually, John decided to sell the LA and Dave travelled to Cornwall with the intention of driving it back to Wakefield. But it didn't turn out that way, recalls Dave. "When I got there, the previous owner fired her up. It sounded fine and a deal was struck. Off we headed, but I ran into trouble around Taunton when there was a loud knocking noise, which seemed to be coming from the Gardner 6LW engine."

Dave managed to limp the Scammell to a nearby services – and it was obvious the engine was not happy. And he was only a mere 300 miles from home!

However, being in the haulage industry helped and a quick phone call summoned

Winching gear was in good condition when truck was bought.

Scammell looks a particularly tough beast front on.

Surely motorists should be honoured to be stuck behind a Scammell, but Dave's message is a nice touch.

Signwriting by the same craftsman who deals with Gee's modern fleet finishes the job.

the Gees' company low-loader, which arrived later in the day.

"It was one of those things. Gardner engines normally give many years of sterling service over thousands of miles. Showmen and fairground operators have always favoured them, not only for powering lorries, but also generators," he says.

The next day back in Yorkshire, Dave investigated the problem. "Number two piston had ploughed a deep groove in the block. It quickly became apparent, once I had split the pistons from the block, that someone had replaced the original Gardner piston with an AES brand unit."

These have a circlip holding the large gudgeon pin in place, whereas the Gardner

has end caps, preventing the piston from rubbing on the sides. The AES circlip had broken away, allowing the gudgeon pin to attack the inside of the cylinder block.

"Finding a good secondhand replacement block was almost impossible, so I had to look for an alternative. Fortunately, I had a good rear block bought at a sale some years ago. I literally cut off the mounting flange, had it machined, and then took it to an engine specialist who stitch-welded it to the front block."

Dave luckily also had some Gardner pistons. "I built up the

Winch and towbar tackle just about anything.

Restoration star Dave Gee in the Scammell's creature comfort-lacking cab.

Front-mounted power winch. The jury's out over whether this was an original feature.

two blocks, connected all the front pipes and injectors, then bolted on the pump, bled some diesel through and pressed the starter button. It fired up, producing that sweet-sounding Gardner roar once again."

Sometimes it's necessary to improvise!

He adds philosophically: "Things are not always as you would expect, and I like to check things over for my own peace of mind." So a thorough inspection of the running gear, brakes and lubricant levels followed.

Although major work was needed to the fuel tank, the Scammell was thankfully in generally good order.

As the Scammell was in a previous owner's livery, he decided to carry out a bare metal repaint. The truck was sandblasted – not an easy task as far as the chassis was concerned because the cab and ballast box were left in situ.

"It meant propping up the Scammell on wooden blocks over a pit. The hardest part of this job is removing all the loose sand from the vehicle. It literally gets everywhere," said Dave. "The only way to do it is to blast the sand away with an air line."

The next task was spraying on the etch primer, again not an easy job chassis-wise with the cab still in place, but as Dave commented, patience is a virtue.

He opted for a Post Office red chassis, with the cab and ballast box in blue – a stunning combination. "It was quite a long process, but I'm pleased with the result," he comments.

Master signwriter Fred Smith did the lettering – his work is featured on all the company's lorries. He also added the White Rose of Yorkshire emblem.

As for the Scammell's early history, one suggestion mentioned earlier is that it may have started off life as a tanker with Esso. However, there are two difficulties with this theory. One is that the original registration number is missing, which means the theory is almost impossible to prove. And we've also heard that this Scammell was not registered for the road for quite a few years – which throws another spanner into the works.

Truck history detectives out there... rally to the cause! Any information on this vehicle's early history, no matter how small, is most welcome.

Normally trusty Gardner suffered problems caused by non-original spec piston.

Scammell stripped for repaint. Sandblasting and painting chassis wasn't an easy task with cab and ballast box in place.

Ballast box contains two tonnes of err... ballast!

Major work was needed to the fuel tank.

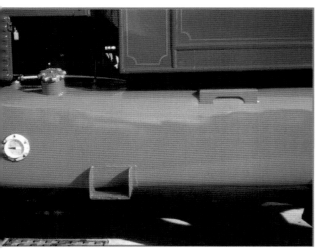

Diesel tank has been extensively repaired.

Scammell with previous owner before front windscreen was converted back to original four-piece style.

(Photos: Glyn Barney)

CIRCLE LIM

A stunning newcomer to this year's rally scene has been an ex-Blue Circle Cement Scammell Routeman owned by Dave Pearson, a driver with the company. We take the beast back to its original depot, hear the full restoration story, and discover another Scammell waiting in the wings!

Nick Larkin reports.

I t's easy to understand why a rock band, fashion model or soap powder has become a household name. But a cement company? Mention Blue Circle to anyone and they'll chirp the word 'cement' back at you. And even someone whose hobby

is flower arranging rather than classic lorries would probably recognise a member of Blue Circle's vivid yellow transport fleet.

Not surprising, then, that one of this year's newcomers to the commercial vehicle rally scene has attracted more attention from Mr and Mrs Public than just about anything else.

ES!

SILO 12

TANKERS ONLY

IN
PC
RM

A

A return to a silo where it often loaded. The silos are loaded from underground, by the way, the cement being blown up into them.

Ram, made by Drum, was in good condition.

Back where it used to be! Scammell Routeman at Blue Circle's Cauldon Works in Staffordshire.

Scammell at Cauldon, Blue Circle contributed towards the restoration.

Blue Circle Cement

WG TANKER GROUP LTD

SCAMMELL

JYM 149W

Dave Pearson's 1981 Scammell Routeman tanker has already taken several awards, but its real accolade is its ability to turn the heads of those whose minds are more likely to be concentrated on whether or not to have fish fingers for tea. Any high street it rumbles through, any retail park it roars past, and people will look.

The rich note of the Leyland TL11 engine also adds to the mixture of course, as does the fact that the vehicle is immaculately clean. Certainly the unmistakable cab design, wonderfully executed by legendary stylist Michelotti, plays a large part. First, it looks like nothing else, so there's more than a hint of nostalgic

recognition, especially around the area in which the Scammell was based.

Secondly – well this is my theory anyway – the cab doesn't have the wide front grille in chrome/black etc as seen on today's vehicles. So it's uncompromisingly yellow. A banana seems blue by comparison. Put this Scammell by its modern equivalent and it doesn't look incredibly dated, just so much more stylish.

Interestingly, plans for this cab go far back as 1961, when Michelotti was working under contract to Leyland. He would design cars such as the Triumph Herald, Spitfire, TR4 and Dolomite. An approach was made to him by Scammell, which had been taken over by Leyland in 1955, and this cab was the result. It was unveiled at the 1962 Motor Show and was used on the Routeman and eventually a variety of other Scammells.

Scammell chassis was in superb condition. Here it is being shotblasted.

Ribbing looks impressive but is a nightmare to paint.

Blue Circle has a long history, the name being created in 1920. The concern actually goes back to the Associated Portland Cement Manufacturers (1900) Ltd. Though today Blue Circle is involved with a diverse range of industry, it will forever be famous for the cement side of the business.

Fleetwise, Foden had been Blue Circle's main supplier for more than 30 years until 1970, when the firm turned its attention to Scammell. By 1977, 750 Routeman were in service, Blue Circle preferring rigids rather than artics, not least because the vehicles would spend much of their time on the often uncertain terrain of quarries and building sites.

Dave Pearson's Scammell, JYW 149W, was among the last batch of 20 Routeman delivered to Blue Circle. Powered by a turbocharged TL11 turbo engine, as fitted to the last 45 Routeman, the Blue Circle examples ran at 30 ton gross.

Dave's vehicle has a six-speed AEC gearbox. The tanker body was made by Metalair, a Blue Circle subsidiary, and has a 20-ton capacity, the Scammell being 30 ton gross.

The vehicle was delivered new to the Blue Circle cement works at Cauldon, Staffs, being based there throughout its working life. It had fleetnumber 2052H, the letter referring to the batch, not the depot.

Dave explains why the Scammell has a London, rather than Staffordshire, registration. "All vehicles at that time were distributed from Blue Circle's central handling workshops Beddington, near Wimbledon. It would have gone there as a chassis and would have the tanks, blowers and mudguards fitted to Blue Circle specification."

The Beddington workshops were in action for more than 50 years and even built the discharge system at the rear of the tanker, which is stamped "Beddington".

JYW 149W remained in service until 1989, in the hands of one driver, Albert Clear. It was then dispatched to Drum Engineering of Bradford, who had it on loan at their development shop for developing new discharge blowers, which are used to discharge the cement from Scammell to silo.

Dave started work at Blue Circle, Cauldon, 10 years ago, though he's been driving lorries since 1969, previously having worked for Shirley's Transport, Stoke-on-Trent, Tideswells at Kingsley, and the now

Owner Dave Pearson ... the Scammell and ... modern steed, a DAF

Discharge unit was made at Blue Circle's Beddington works.

Scammell styling extended to the door trims.

defunct printers and dyers, Thomas, Arthur Wardle of Leek.

"The Scammells had all gone by the time I arrived at Blue Circle. We were on the roadtrains then, but drivers still had fond memories of the Routeman."

Dave, who had always been a Scammell fan, heard about the vehicle being at Drum's Bradford works. "I went there on the Saturday morning, found out where it was, photographed it, and had to have it."

The Scammell was towed back to Dave's Staffordshire base, where he succumbed to the temptation of a short test drive.

"Took us about two or three hours to get the fuel through and it eventually started. I took it for a run up the yard just to try it. By the time I'd done that, four or five air pipes burst, the air packs were leaking and it was a case of parking it up and starting from scratch."

Thankfully, the engine and turbo were in excellent condition. The brakes were stripped, three new chambers being needed, and all the air pipes were replaced with plastic units, as seen on modern vehicles. The wheels were removed, the chassis was shotblasted and painted. The fibreglass cab had remained in reasonable condition, though some minor filling was needed.

The tanker body had survived well, but new outlet pipes were needed – the discharge unit actually being made at the Blue Circle workshops and carrying the description "Beddington".

The tipping mechanism worked well; it takes about two minutes to fully raise the tank.

As far as loading and unloading is concerned, the tanker is loaded from the top, and when the body is tipped up, the cement goes to the end of the tanker. Air is blown in from the discharge unit at the back and the tanker body acts like a chimney, the cement rising into the silo.

Body repainting was carried out by commercial vehicle painter Mick Davis, from Ashbourne, Derbyshire, using polyurethane paint, a superb job particularly as the Michelotti cab, with its styling ridges, is not the easiest of subjects.

Blue Circle provided much assistance in the restoration, providing the paint and contributing towards the cost of the repaint. The company also found and donated a set of transfers.

"Putting these on a tanker would be a nightmare, and it was best to get professional help here." Dave remembers. Easyfix Emblems of Leek did the job.

WG Tankers of Cauldon, which maintains Blue Circle's tankers,

contributed towards the repaint and provided mudguards. "The originals were plastic with a tin top. I couldn't get any of these anywhere, and so the replacement are steel."

Dave would like to thank both organisations for their assistance, and everyone else who helped with the project

John Ferns, a driver for Blue Circle and expert electrician, tackled the electrics. "Over the years they had left wires here and there, cut wires and made other alterations, but overall the electrics weren't in too bad a condition," recalls Dave.

There was one major problem: "The French Cibie headlights were difficult to get hold of. Apparently they were the same as on a Vauxhall Viva, but they were concave, not convex." Eventually, Lancashire-based Chorley Electrics managed to source a new set of lights.

The interior has worn well, though Dave has just sourced a new headlining.

So after much work and two new tyres being fitted, one immaculate Scammell was ready for action, the result of a two-year project. Its first rally was the 2001 Llandudno event.

"We finally got it finished on the Friday night – Llandudno started on the Saturday. It wasn't even MoT'd until the Friday afternoon." The Scammell

The second Scammell is in surprisingly good condition. It's expected to be restored as a flatbed.

...ammell number 2 in action. It may look like a vehicle from Mad Max, but runs well, although the engine breathes a bit. The exhaust stack was fitted during the vehicle's quarry work era.

...heir heyday - Routeman line-up at Cauldon for ... publicity shot. These earlier vehicles ran at 24 tons gross.

...erformed admirably on its long journey to ...ales, and cruises around 50mph.

The Scammell went on to pick up awards at ...e CVRTC Gaydon event. So how does Dave ...m up the Routeman's appeal? "It's great to ...rive, the Michelotti styling is superb... and it's ... Blue Circle Scammell!"

But Dave's Scammell story doesn't end with ...YW 149W. He now has a sister Routeman, ...inus tanker, registration HYK 612W, ...eetnumber 1868X. Another ex-Cauldon ...ehicle, this machine had spent its latter days as ... water bowser on the nearby quarry.

"They'd stopped using it and bought a ...umptruck instead. I took pity on it, to be ...onest. I convinced myself I needed a Scammell ...or spares, but, considering the time it's spent at ...e quarry, it's survived well and is even a good ...unner, though the engine breathes a bit."

Dave's intention is to ...onvert this second Scammell ...to a flatbed, complete with a suitable load of cement bags. "They had five of these at Cauldon, and as far as we know, no originals survive."

Talking of survival, you may well be wondering why there are no ex-Blue Circle Scammells around, either on the rally circuit or anywhere else for that matter. There's a simple, if excruciating explanation. Blue Circle was notorious for cutting holes in the tankers and slicing the chassis of its redundant vehicles before scrapping them – so they didn't fall into the hands of competitors.

Today, the Scammells and Leylands are replaced by DAFs, and Cauldon only has some 20 lorries in its fleet. Changes in cement distribution, including a policy of offering discounts to bulk customers who arranged their own collection, meant a rapid reduction in the fleet, which at its peak was around 1600 vehicles and is now less than a quarter of that.

Not all is lost, however. Dave, who also owns a magnificent 1942 Diamond T, has discovered that Blue Circle still has a couple of Scammells used on internal work at another Midlands site. "I've definitely got my eye on those, so watch this space!"

> * Many thanks to Blue Circle for allowing us to photograph the Scammell at Cauldon.

Scammell cruises around 50mph on the road.

...re's one we restored earlier...

ARTIC EIGHT

by Mike Jeffries

United Dairies were a big user of Scammell artics long before the articulated vehicles became popular in general haulage in the 1960s. Gardner-powered with the tricky Scammell six-speed constant mesh gearbox, this 1948 example had a long life of over twenty years.

A laser print of this image is available from Mike on 01803 882067.
His website is www.transportart.co.uk.

Selling the Scammell Commai

In the first of an occasional series, we take a look at the fascinating world of military-vehicle sales

DURING the 50 or so years which elapsed between 1932 and 1984, the British Army employed just three types of heavy tank transporter in quantity - the 30-ton Scammell Pioneer, the 40-ton Diamond T Model 980/981, and the 40/50-ton Thornycroft Antar, through Marks 1, 2 and 3 (FV12000 series). By the mid-sixties it was becoming obvious that the Antar, even in what had become its latest Rolls-Royce powered Mk 3/3A guise, was becoming rather too long in the tooth, and the Ministry of Defence (MoD) began casting around for a replacement.

Military opinion on the question of tank-transporter design swings from one extreme to the other - one minute only a specialised vehicle will do, and then the inevitable horrendous cost suggests that perhaps there might be a suitable tractor on the civilian market. In the late sixties, the Ministry believed that the military requirements for heavy transporter trains were unique, and that suitable commercial vehicles were not suitable. So, although inevitably this brought with it a high price, the Ministry resolved that the new tank transporter would have to be purpose-designed. In 1968, an outline specification was drawn up and put out to tender to Scammell and Thornycroft. This may seem strange for both companies had been owned by Leyland for some years, but the Group encouraged them to compete in the market and both pitched for the work.

The Thornycroft bid was successful and the company was awarded the development contract for the Army's new tank transporter, at that time rated at 55 tons. Development of what at first was known as the Thornycroft Mighty Antar Mk 4 began in a half-hearted way in late 1968, but there was little real progress and the Ministry seemed to be dragging its feet.

As soon as the three Commander engineering models were complete, Scammell produced this splendid poster/brochure which featured the Iranian tractor with the early Cranes 55-ton MoD semi-trailer.

Scammell

For over half a century, Scammell has been one of the great names in road transport – a reputation established as early as 1919 and consolidated by a series of classic vehicle designs reaching up to the present day.

The Scammell heritage began in the Victorian era, when the name was associated with craftsman-built carts and vans. When the horse gave way to the internal combustion engine, Scammell's business moved with the times and – as in so many other fields – the 1914-18 war provided a forcing house for progress.

The war years left no doubt of the value and efficiency of motor transport, but it was not until 1919 that the name of Scammell was established in its own right. In that year, Scammell pioneered the concept of articulated vehicles when the company's first "artic" pulled a trailer load of nearly 8 tons up a steep London hill.

In 1922, Scammell Lorries Limited was formally incorporated with the object of developing and marketed articulated vehicles. By 1927, Scammell had strengthened its position by launching its first cross-country tank transporter, aptly named the Pioneer, and two years later the Company introduced the world's largest truck, the "Hundred-Tonner" heavy haulage tractor.

In 1933, Scammell's leadership was enhanced by the introduction of the "Mechanical Horse", a 3-wheel tractor with articulated trailer which, with its automatic coupling and ability to turn in less than its own length, set new standards of versatility in road transport. Over 20,000 of these 3-ton (3.05 tonne) tractors were built.

During World War 2, Scammell made a massive contribution to the war effort, building large numbers of tank transporters, gun tractors and Pioneer heavy recovery vehicles – some of which are still in service in various countries of the world today.

After the war, Scammell developed three and four-axled heavy trucks of the rigid type and two and three-axled tractor units with a complete range of semi-trailers. These included patented frameless tanker semi-trailers for all types of liquids, from water and spirit through to hot chocolate and corrosives.

The company also found itself increasingly involved in such fields as heavy construction, oil drilling, mining and logging, with vehicles such as the 6 x 6 Explorer, 4 x 4 Mountaineer and, by 1952, the Constructor – forerunner of today's cross-country heavies. Later in the 1950s the Super Constructor was introduced, followed by the 4 x 2 Highwayman, 6 x 4 Junior Constructor, 4 x 2 Sherpa dump-truck, and 6 x 4 Himalayan dump-truck.

The start of the 1960s was marked by the introduction of the 4 x 2 Handyman series and maxi-mum-length semi-trailers, 6 x 4 and, later, 6 x 2 Trunker series and 6 x 4 Routeman. In 1965, the 6 x 4 Contractor heavy-haulage prime-mover went into production. Over the next few years, other designs were introduced, and in 1969 the 6 x 4 Crusader made its bow.

During the early 1970's a 4 x 2 version of the Crusader was brought into production. In the mid 70's Scammell was busy on production of the 6 x 4 Crusader for the Royal Engineers and Royal Corps of Transport, over 300 entering service. Development work continued on the Contractor, which was fitted with the 625 bhp Cummins engine with Allison fully automatic transmission.

Since 1977, one of the main developments has been the Nubian range of 6 x 6 and 4 x 4 rear-engine fire crash tender chassis which capitalise on the experience of the leading UK manufacturer of crash tender systems.

Today, the Scammell reputation for innovation and advance is maintained by the Commander tank transporter. Designed for the transport of main battle-tanks of up to 65 tonnes weight, this rugged vehicle is powered by a turbocharged and after-cooled 625 bhp Rolls-Royce V12 engine. It provides hill climb and acceleration comparable to that of a 32.5 tonns (32 ton) gross combination weight articulated vehicle. The vehicle is also engineered for installation of the Cummins KTA600 engine.

Scammell builds all vehicles to the exacting quality standards of the Ministry of Defence standards DEF-STAN 05/21. This level of quality is good practice throughout Scammell's design workshop, assembly and administrative organisation.

1927 – The first Scammell tank transporter.
1978 – The Scammell "Commander" tank transporter

ler

Right and below: The Iranian tractor was put through trials at the MoD Bagshot and Farnborough test sites before being shipped to Teheran. These views also show the special semi-trailer which was intended for Iran.

When vehicle production was terminated at the Thornycroft factory in 1971, the work moved, along with most of the design team, to Scammell's Watford factory, and for a while the project was known as the Contractor Mk 3. In 1976, Scammell was officially appointed as prime contractor for the completion of the work.

At the same time, Scammell had been negotiating to supply a similar tank transporter and semi-trailer to the Iranian government, and in 1977 set-up a joint venture with Rolls-Royce for the completion

of this project. The intention was that the vehicle would be supplied in knocked-down form for local assembly - Rolls-Royce were even proposing to establish an engine factory in Teheran. The basic design parameters, which were very similar to those for the MoD vehicle, had already been defined and Scammell had constructed a full-sized wooden mock-up for Iran in 1976. The similarity between the two projects meant that the mock-up helped to shorten the development cycle for the MoD tractor, and by 1977/78 the company was in a

position to construct three basically-similar engineering models: two were for the MoD, the third was for Iran. The Iranian tractor was shipped to Teheran and put through desert trials.

Having got the project through the drawing-board stages and into (albeit limited) reality, the prospect of other, lucrative export sales loomed. Believing that they had a world-class tank transporter on their hands, the marketing boys got to work producing a sales leaflet. The Iranian tractor was bulled-up and photographed and took pride of place on the front of a lavish A1-sized full-colour brochure/poster - remarkably similar to the leaflet you might expect to pick-up at the local British Leyland dealer for a Maxi or Allegro. Unfortunately there were no takers. But nevertheless, the Commander was the last purpose-designed heavy military Scammell, and the company remained hopeful that once it went into production, overseas sales would surely follow.

When the Shah of Iran was toppled by the Ayatollah Khomeni's regime in 1979, the country's preferences for military-equipment procurement turned to the East, and the Iranian Commander project was cancelled - and the engineering model which had been sent to Iran for sales disappeared along with any remaining hope of export sales in that particular market. Scammell and the MoD were left to go it alone.

Back in Britain, the path to completion remained rocky and hazardous, and the MoD version of the Commander was cancelled twice under Maggie Thatcher's

In early June 1984, Major General Whalley (Director General, Ordnance Services, RCT) handed the keys of the first production Commander to Major General Derrick Braggins (Director General, Transport & Movements, RCT).

Scammell team, nor to keep the proverbial wolf from the Watford door.

The factory was hungry for work, and the Scammell management team still believed that the vehicle had enormous potential. After all, it had actually started life as a tank transporter for Iran, and had already been tested satisfactorily under the harshest desert conditions, so clearly there was export potential.

In 1984, the Commander (which was coded S25 by Scammell) was included in the company's 'general' tank-transporter brochure, alongside the S24 and S26 commercial vehicles which were also being sold for tank-transporter duties. But where these latter models were essentially off-the-shelf products, the Commander was a purpose-built military truck powered by a hugely-expensive Rolls-Royce CV12 engine. Scammell were up against the far slicker, and probably far-more heavily-supported sales operations of the American truck manufacturers, and unfortunately it seems that no-one was prepared to buy a Scammell when they could have a big Mack or an Oshkosh. Undaunted, the company still believed that the Middle East was a prime opportunity, and in 1987, a simple leaflet was produced in Arabic describing the basic technical specification of the Commander. I've seen more lavish leaflets for an Indian take-away so perhaps it is not surprising that it produced no new takers for what was a quarter-of-a-million pound tank transporter.

Finally, events overtook Scammell, and in 1988 British Leyland closed the factory, selling the rights to manufacture the Commander, as well as to supply spares, to

budget cuts of the 'seventies. However, seemingly against all odds, the vehicle finally went into production in 1983 with the first of just 125 examples being delivered in February 1984. By the time production commenced, the Ministry of Defence had paid close to £1,500,000 for the development work, and was committed to paying a price of £218,000 each for the production of 125 examples. However, by this time losses in the Austin-Rover car-making divisions of the Group meant that both Leyland and Scammell were in deep difficulties, and the total income to the company of some £4.2 million for sales to the MoD was not felt to be sufficient to fully justify the effort that had been put into the vehicle by the

Peter Rotheroe's Unipower operation. Unfortunately there was still no queue of eager buyers, and although Unipower did comprehensively rebuild a handful of the badly-damaged Gulf War veterans, badging at least one of them 'Unipower', no more Commanders were constructed and none entered service with any other country.

The Commander continues to appear in Jane's 'Military vehicles and logistics', and in other industry directories, albeit now identified as a Unipower product (produced by Alvis-Unipower from 1996), but there is no longer any possibility of further sales. In fact, Unipower launched a new 75-tonne 8x8 tank transporter as part of their 'M Series' family of medium-mobility heavy vehicles in 1995, supplying a number to Oman, and in 1997 pitching it as part of a 'PFI' all-in package to the MoD for the replacement of the Commander. The bid was not successful and the Unipower operation is now up for sale by its owners, Alvis.

So, although it acquitted itself superbly in the Gulf War and has provided extraordinary value-for-money to the MoD, no-one else ever did buy the Commander. Now into their third decade of service, the British Army continues to operate them, and for the collector and enthusiast they are a regular, and very fine sight on the roads. I wonder what will happen to them when the fifth-generation of British tank transporter (which is being supplied by the American company Oshkosh) starts to displace the mighty Commander... will some well-heeled enthusiast be brave enough to step in where the Ayatollah Khomeni feared to tread?

Right: In late 1984, the Commander was included in Scammell's general tank-transporter brochure alongside the commercially-derived S24 and S26 tractors.

Left and above: In 1987, Scammell Special Trucks, as it had been renamed, produced this simple A4 brochure in English and Arabic describing what was essentially the standard British Army 65-tonne Commander and Cranes semi-trailer.

The Commander is designed as a complete operating unit for the transportation of main battle tanks up to 64 tonnes in weight. The unit is capable of starting and operating in a temperature range from −24°C to 43°C, anywhere up to 500m above sea level.

The fully laden unit is capable of maintaining a continuous operational speed of 62kph and climbing a 20% gradient. It will also stop, hold and restart on this gradient. The unit will ford, unprepared, a river up to a depth of 760mm and negotiate a T intersection of 9.15m between walls.

Just 125 examples of the definitive 65-tonne Scammell Commander were produced and supplied to the British Army; following mine and accident damage in the Gulf in 1991, only 120 remain.

The Pion

Pat Ware takes a nostalgic look at Scammell's 'big friendly giant'

On the face of it, whilst it is easy to see the connections between say MG, Jaguar and Ferrari, add Jeep and Scammell to the mix and they appear to have little in common. But scratch under the skin a little and you will find that these companies are all members of that select band of motor manufacturers for which there is universal respect and recognition.

As a truly independent truck designer, and manufacturer of what were possibly Britain's finest heavy commercial vehicles, Scammell has been gone for some 20 years. Even the name has not appeared on new vehicles since the late 'eighties. And yet, unaccountably, the magic in the name appears to survive, and 'Scammell' still seems to have the power to make grown men go misty-eyed and talk longingly about the massive Constructors, Explorers, Highwaymen and Contractors that once stalked the world's highways...

Standing head and shoulders above even these monsters is the old 'War Department' Pioneer.

The Pioneer was a product of the late 'twenties which somehow survived through the next four decades. It was slow and underpowered, it had no front-wheel brakes, and was blessed with a truly antique 'perpendicular' cab, open to the elements on both sides. Even in 1942, let alone at the end of the War, the Pioneer was overshadowed in every respect, except perhaps character, by more modern and capable American machines. The company slogan might have said 'when the going gets tough only a Scammell is good enough' but the truth is that it was scarcely able to hold its

own against the Mighty Mack, the flashy Diamond T and the formidable Dragon Wagon. The only positive thing that could truly be said about the Pioneer at the time was that it was reliable.

And yet, when you look at the Pioneer through the rose-tinted glasses of nostalgia you can see that it has a certain, indefinable 'something'. Like a big old dog it seems friendly, eager and unthreatening - it looks like it wants to please... and in case you think I'm beginning to lose my grip on reality, I'd like you to know that I'm not alone in this view of the beast.

In 1935, the Royal Artillery started to take delivery of the Scammell Pioneer R100 heavy artillery tractor. Typical loads included the 5.5in, 7.2in and 8in Howitzers, 6in heavy artillery piece and 4.5in anti-aircraft gun.

REME used the Pioneer for 25 or more years after the War and the crewmen almost universally regarded it like a family pet.

Designed by Scammell's talented Chief Engineer, Oliver Danson North, development of the Pioneer started in 1925. It was intended for use as an oilfield tractor, where by virtue of a unique suspension system, its formidable performance on un-made roads was a positive virtue. The company achieved considerable commercial success with overseas operators who needed a truck which could boldly go where unsurfaced roads were the norm... but, save for one sale to the Indian Army in 1929, Scammell were unable to break into what they saw as the

eer spirit

This is the heavy recovery tractor variant, deliveries of which started in 1936. The photograph shows the SV/2S version which had a suspended-tow capacity of 3-8 tons according to the jib extension.

SV/2S heavy recovery tractor in its post-war deep-bronze green finish.

SV/2S heavy recovery tractor in its post-war deep-bronze green finish.

lucrative military market.

In 1928, the War Office had dipped a toe into the water, purchasing and testing a 6x4 Pioneer-based armoured car (well, actually it was a wooden mock-up of an armoured car but let's not get picky). It was not successful, and following some initial trials, the project was abandoned. During the same year, the War Office also purchased a standard 6x6 Pioneer and put it through a series of trials designed to test its suitability as a heavy artillery tractor. It was pitched head-to-head against the standard AEC/FWD R6T 6x6 tractor and was felt, not only to be inferior, but also to be unreliable.

And

finally, in 1932 the War Office realised that the massive Pioneer might also make a useful tank transporter, and presumably the sales team at Scammell believed that the War Office was getting serious at last. Another contract was issued, this time for a 6x4 Pioneer tractor equipped with a special 16/18-ton low-loading semi-trailer suitable for carrying the relatively-lightweight tanks of the period. But it was to be another false dawn. Although the tank transporter was used for trials and demonstrations, apparently the War Office felt they had no need for more than one of these new-fangled tank transporters and no more orders were forthcoming. That is until Hitler started throwing

this weight around. In 1937, rather too late in the day as it proved, the War Office realised that perhaps the tanks might not be able to drive all the way to France, and the first real production contract was placed with Scammell for a handful of 20-ton semi-trailer tank transporters, designated TRMU20. Further orders followed for this, and for an uprated, 30-ton variant (TRMU30) but at the outbreak of War, there was just a handful of vehicles available.

The Royal Artillery meanwhile had also been buying Pioneers for use as a heavy artillery tractor (R100) and, since their order had been placed in 1935, it took precedence over the tank-transporter variant in Scammell's over-committed production schedule. And similarly, the RASC, and later REME, specified the Scammell Pioneer chassis for use as a heavy recovery tractor and deliveries of this variant (SV1S, SV2S) started in 1936.

Aside from a handful of experimental vehicles, all of the military Pioneers shared the same basic 6x4 chassis design and the same automotive components. Power was provided by the superb Gardner 6LW diesel engine, driving the rear wheels only through Scammell's six-speed gearbox with its distinctive open gate. The unique

In 1932, the War Office purchased one 6x4 Scammell Pioneer, together with a 16/18 ton low-loader semi-trailer, for trials as a tank transporter.

Left: The normal WW2 finish was matt green which weathers to this greeny-grey; note that this vehicle has an anti-aircraft hip ring on the cab roof.

Below: Head-on view of the R100 artillery tractor.

The recovery tractors were fitted with these substantial brackets ahead of the radiator designed to allow counterweights to be used to prevent the front wheels leaving the road during suspended-towing operations.

combination of a walking-beam gearcase system at the rear and centrally-pivoting axle at the front provided incredible axle movement and articulation, and whilst it was by no means an off-road vehicle, this arrangement at least ensured that the Pioneer's big balloon tyres were able to maintain contact with the ground regardless of the terrain. No attempt was made to update the vehicle's appearance, and the axle-forward design and flat-panelled cab were throwbacks to the origins of the vehicle 10 years previously. Aside from the bodywork, obviously there were detail differences to suit the particular application, for example the tank transporter was constructed on a longer wheelbase chassis and was equipped with lower ratios in the final drive.

Despite working flat out on Ministry contracts for the duration of the War, it would be fair to say that Scammell simply could not cope with the demand: total production of the military Pioneers was 3572; 574 of these were tank transporters, 980 artillery tractors, and 2018 of the recovery variant. This was never enough, and for the entire duration of the War there was a shortage of heavy tractors, and particularly of the tank-transporter variant... and, 'God bless America' - for without the Diamond T, Mack, Kenworth and Ward LaFrance heavy tractors the British Army would have surely been struggling. With WW2 out of the way, the War

Office was able to sit back and re-appraise the entire military-vehicle fleet. Neither the 20- or 30-ton tank transporters had ever really been adequate, and many were de-mobbed immediately; others were converted to ballast tractors simply because there remained a shortage of such machines. The civilian market loved them, with battered old war-weary examples finding their way onto the fairground, and into the heavy-haulage and road-making sectors where plodding reliability was prized

beyond maximum loading capacity. The R100 artillery tractors remained on strength until they started to be superseded in the mid-fifties by the FV1100 Leyland Martian series, while the recovery vehicles were considered to be so good that REME seemed truly sorry to see the last one go in 1965. Despite the appearance of the FV1119 recovery variant of the FV1100 series, the REME recovery crews seemed to prefer the old Pioneer which appeared to provide just the right combination of technical simplicity and pulling power. De-mobbed recovery tractors were also snapped up by the civilian market and for years it was not uncommon to see a trusty Pioneer hard at work on the motorway trying to sort out some difficult heavy recovery task. It was simple, reliable and powerful.

When the time came round again for the

Although it is open to the rear, the cab of the tank transporter is designed to provide accommodation for seven men, allowing the crew of the transporter and the AFV load to travel in relative comfort.

The early production tank transporters were rated at 20 tons but this was soon uprated to 30 tons; this photograph shows the 30-ton variant with the early semi-trailer which had a single slope to the load bed.

The artillery tractor was fitted with a steel-panelled rear body designed to provide accommodation for the gun crew and to allow ammunition and other equipment to be carried.

Technical specification

Engine: Gardner 6LW diesel; six cylinder; 8396cc; overhead valves; power output 102bhp at 1700rpm.
Transmission: 6F1R; 6x4.
Suspension: centrally-pivoted front axle carried on transverse leaf spring; walking-beam gearcases at the rear on semi-elliptical springs.
Brakes: air-pressure.
Construction: steel ladder chassis with coach-built timber-framed cab panelled in steel; rear body in steel or timber according to application.
Electrical system: nominal 12V wired in series/parallel to give 24V for starting.

Dimensions (tractor only)
Length: tank transporter (tractor only), 275in; artillery tractor, 243in; recovery tractor, 240in.
Width: tank transporter, 96in; artillery tractor and recovery tractor, 102in.
Height: tank transporter and recovery tractor, 113in; artillery tractor, 117in.
Wheelbase: tank transporter, 180in; artillery tractor and recovery tractor, 146in.
Weight: 20-ton tank transporter (tractor only), 23,380 lb; 30-ton tank transporter (tractor only), 25,985 lb; artillery tractor, 18,750 lb; recovery tractor, 21,644 lb.

Variants
Tractor, 6x4, heavy, Scammell (model designation, R100)
Tractor, 6x4, breakdown, heavy, Scammell (model designation, SV1T, SV1S and SV2S)
Transporter, 6x4, 20 ton, 6x4+8, semi-trailer recovery, Scammell (model designation, TRMU20/TRCU20)
Transporter, 6x4, 30 ton, 6x4+8, semi-trailer recovery, Scammell (model designation, TRMU30/TRCU30)

old Pioneers to be pensioned off, many found their way onto the collectors' market. As you might expect, although there are few tank transporters and artillery tractors in preservation, the SV2S recovery tractor has probably survived in greater numbers than any other British heavy military vehicle.

And perhaps it's not so hard to see why....

Regardless of its date of delivery, the military Pioneer is essentially a pre-war truck - to the collector this is a positive advantage. On the road the Pioneer's top speed is just 15 or 24 miles an hour - it doesn't matter how hard you press your foot to the floor, that's all she'll do - 15 miles an hour for the tank transporter, 24 for the artillery and recovery tractors. There are no front-wheel brakes, so emergency stops can be a chancy business - although you could argue that with a maximum top speed of, yes 15 or 24 miles an hour, 'emergency' stops are unlikely to be called for and that it hardly matters. Apart from a four-piece windscreen,

there are no proper windows, so the antique cab is open and draughty, dating from a time when 'ergonomic' was little more than a word in the dictionary. But of course, for antique, read 'character'. There is no power assistance on the steering so cornering the beast is hard work... and it's huge, uncomfortable and noisy. Again, these things can be considered to add to the fun for the military-vehicle collector, and driving Pioneer means that you are always literally at the head of the queue...

The Pioneer is still spoken of in almost hushed and reverend tones, with present-day owners appearing to belong to a very exclusive club. At shows, Pioneers attract enthusiasts like bees round the proverbial honeypot. Even old RASC tank-transporter drivers hark back nostalgically to their days behind the wheel of the Scammell in the Western Desert. Some dismiss the upstart Diamond T and talk fondly of the old Pioneer as though it were in every way superior... one old soldier I spoke to told me

he 'wouldn't be able to afford the bus fare to the radiator of the Diamond T to check the water'.

Hindsight is a wonderful thing isn't it!

Very few tank transporters have made it into preservation; this 30-ton example is the only one known to have survived with the correct semi-trailer. It is finished in post-war deep-bronze green.

THE EARLY PIONEERS

The editor looks at Britain's first purpose-built tank transporte

In the 50 or so years between 1932 and 1984, Scammell Lorries of Watford supplied the British Army with more than 700 tank transporters, by far the largest number of which were the famous 20- and 30-ton Pioneers of WW2, but the number also includes 122 production examples of the 98-tonne Commander which remains in service to this day. But most significantly, it was Scammell which supplied the Army with its very first purpose-built tank transporter in 1932 - a 6x4 Pioneer-based tractor with a permanently-coupled 16/18-ton low-loading semi-trailer.

Oliver Danson North, Scammell's brilliant designer and engineer, had joined the company in 1923 and by 1925

he had started work with Percy G Hugh on what was to become the Pioneer, with the first prototype produced in 1927. By the standards of the day it was a most impressive machine consisting of a substantial 6x4 chassis powered by a Scammell 7-litre petrol engine producing 53bhp; the drive was transmitted through a four-speed Scammell gearbox to a massive worm-drive rear axle produced by Kirkstall Forge Engineering. But, of course, the most impressive feature was the extraordinary suspension. At the rear, the centrally-pivoted walking-beam gearcases carrying the rear wheels were able to assume extreme angles of articulation relative to one another, with almost a foot of movement available in the vertical plane. The front suspension

was no less innovative and the, usually undriven, front axle was centrally pivote and suspended by means of a transverse elliptical spring giving two-feet of movement from bump to rebound. The chassis rode on huge straight-sided Goodyear pneumatic balloon tyres with an external diameter of 44 inches.

All of these features conspired to provide the Pioneer with a plodding, unstoppable performance which was we suited to unmade or poorly-made roads and which would literally allow the vehicle to climb walls. And clearly these

Below: The tank transporter and semi-trailer under test by Scammell; the load consists of a solid-tyred trailer ballasted to 17 tons.

Below: Although this is not actually one series of photographs, since the load is variously a Mk 1 and Mk 3 Vickers medium tank, it does nicely show the loading sequence. The first step was to lower the trailer to the ground, via the jacks, and to remove the rear bogie; once the bogie was safely out of the way, the tank could be driven or winched onto the trailer; the trailer bogie was rolled back into position, attached to the lugs on the trailer and laboriously raised via the screw jacks (in the twin tubes seen between the wheels); once the bogie was locked back in position and the brake lines coupled up, the outfit was ready to roll.

Above: The vehicle as it appeared in Army service, complete with a Vickers Mk 1 medium tank load. Note the fancy cast spoked wheels.

Right: Scammell brochure from April 1935 - it includes photographs of the civilian Pioneers as well as the military artillery tractors and the prototype tank transporter.

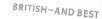

Scammell PIONEER goes where no other vehicle has been

...irtues were exactly what were to ...ventually endear it to a generation of ...ilitary users.

Almost immediately, two vehicles went ...ff to Venezuela where they were put to ...ork on the oilfields; a 6x6 version was ...upplied to the Indian Army for use as a ...un tractor; and 21 tractors with skeleton ...emi-trailers were purchased by the Iraq ...etroleum Company (IPC) for hauling ...teel pipelines across the Mosul oilfield. ...n 1928/29, a short-wheelbase chassis was ...upplied to the War Office for possible ...se as an armoured car and a mock-up ...ooden body was constructed for it; a ...econd chassis was supplied for ...onsideration as a gun tractor at about the ...ame time. In late 1931, Scammell ...rranged a demonstration of three 6x4 ...ioneers to the Australian Gold Mining ...ompany. The demonstration was held at ...venue described as being 'a short ...istance from Watford' which, judging by ...e photographs, would appear to have ...een the Bagshot proving ground of the ...heeled Vehicles Experimental ...stablishment (WVEE) so it would be ...urprising if some Army observers were ...ot present. The vehicles acquitted ...emselves extremely well and ...ontemporary trade press reports were ...ositively lyrical about the Pioneer's ...erformance.

It was possibly as a result of these ...emonstrations that the War

Office decided to purchase one example of the Scammell Pioneer equipped with a 16/18-ton low-loading semi-trailer designed for transporting the Vickers medium tank. It was purchased under contract V2327 and was described as a 'transporter, heavy, 10-wheeled', and was allocated the War Office census number T22509, which identified it as though it were a tank. Like all military vehicles of this inter-war period, it was also given a civilian registration number, in this case MV 5364, a London series issued between 1931 and 1933.

With hindsight, it seems strange that just one vehicle was purchased but let's consider for a moment what had brought the War Office to recognise that perhaps

it had a need for a purpose-built tank transporter. During the Great War, the tanks had been moved either by rail or on their tracks - however, even modern tanks do not respond kindly to travelling any great distance on metalled roads, and back then the machines were notoriously unreliable, exhibiting high levels of wear and tear, and frequently shedding or breaking tracks.

Below: Here's the whole rig, loaded and ready to move out.

IWM, KID2760

IWM, KID2793, 3821, 3989, 4093, 4527

Technical specification

Nomenclature: transporter, heavy, 10-wheeled, 16 tons; Scammell Pioneer.

Engine: Scammell; four-cylinders; 7000cc; side valves; power output 53bhp at 2000rpm.
Transmission: 5F1R; 6x4.
Suspension: centrally-pivoted front axle, suspended on transverse semi-elliptical spring; single rear axle with walking-beam oscillating gear cases suspended on semi-elliptical springs.
Brakes: mechanical by rods and cable, with air assistance; on rear wheels of tractor and on trailer only
Construction: steel ladder chassis; steel-panelled cab on timber frame; semi-trailer of riveted construction.
Electrical system: 6V.

Dimensions
Length, 599in overall; tractor only, 258in. Width, 108in. Height, 114in. Wheelbase, 523in overall; tractor only, 181in; bogie centres, 55in. Weight, 33,460 lb.

Clearly there was a need for some means of moving the tanks but, remember, motor transport was still in its infancy and steam traction engines remained the primary method of heavy haulage. However, unless the boiler was constantly maintained at pressure, which meant keeping the fire in continuously, they were not available for immediate deployment and anyway, were slow and difficult to conceal from the enemy - and, their huge iron wheels and primitive or non-existent suspension were scarcely suited to off-road use anyway. The Fowler Lion traction engine, for example, was capable of hauling 50 tons, but no photographs appear to exist of traction engines carrying tanks, so perhaps even the conservative chaps in charge at the War Office had finally embraced the idea that steam traction was a thing of the past. Immediately after the end of the Great War, AEC supplied the War Office with a number of 'K Type' chain-drive 4x2 trucks which had been modifed to couple to a Bauly semi-trailer rated at 12 tons. Although these were actually intended to carry the Holt tractor, it must have been obvious that they could also carry the lighter tanks, and in 1928 one was demonstrated with a Vickers medium tank as a load.

The four-wheeled 16/18-ton semi-trailer was of riveted construction and was coupled to the tractor via a Scammell coupling.

Its progress was slow and ungainly, but it did at least offer a way forward, and a year later, the War Office purchased a commercial Scammell eight-wheeled articulated outfit and ran trials with this as a tank transporter, concluding that it provided better performance than the AEC. However, things still remained fluid, for later that year a 16-ton iron-wheeled trailer was developed as a possible prototype for recovering disabled tanks from the battlefield. There were actually two alternative designs put forward but neither would have been particularly convenient to operate - one, for example, requiring both axles to be removed to allow loading. The Army still lacked a sufficiently-powerful wheeled tractor and it is unclear how the trailer might have been towed.

However, despite the inevitable budgetary constraints, the War Office was moving inexorably towards purchasing some form of motorised tank transporter/recovery vehicle and the impressive demonstrations of the Pioneer's performance off road may well

have tipped the balance. Clearly the first Pioneer was purchased simply as an experiment - a brave step forward into the unknown.

With its big six-wheeled tractor and four-wheeled low-loading semi-trailer, the outfit was surprisingly close to the modern conception of the motorised tank transporter - there was even a winch mounted behind the cab to assist in recovering disabled tanks. Power was provided by the Scammell petrol engine driving through a five-speed Scammell gearbox to the single rear axle with its innovative oscillating gearcases.

It could be argued that this primitive tank transporter set the pattern for all such vehicles for the next 50 years - the definitive wartime Pioneer, the Thornycroft Antar of the 'fifties, the Scammell Commander of the 'eighties, and the soon-to be delivered Oshkosh M1097E all follow the same general layout.

However, there was still a way to go with the semi-trailer.

The trailer was rated at a respectable 16/18 tons, and was carried on a single, removable, four-wheeled bogie at the rear and attached to the tractor by means of a Scammell coupling - something like a huge ball joint. The chassis was of riveted construction and consisted of twin longitudinal main members joined and braced by a series of flanged cross members; a swan neck at the front carried the frame up and over the coupling to the tractor. The gently-sloping flat load bed was provided with twin runways, with space for tool and

IWM, KID4072

IWM, KID2679

Left: The trailer was free to turn through more than 180° relative to the tractor.

Below: This view shows the tractor-mounted winch, which was used to load disabled AFVs and the spring-loaded rear tow hook. Note how the tank is pulled sufficiently hard up against the trailer swan neck that the tracks are slightly deformed.

quipment stowage between the runways nd cross members. On the downside, the ailer was hugely disadvantaged by aving no loading ramps and must have een extraordinarily slow and difficult to perate. The bogie was provided with win screw jacks in tall cylindrical posts ehind the rear wheels; these supported ne trailer deck, and in order to effect ading and unloading, the deck had to be wered to the ground by means of these crew jacks and then detached from its cating sockets. Once the bogie was moved it could be manhandled out of e way and the tank loaded onto the ailer. Once the tank was in position and shed down, the bogie was moved back to position, attached to the locating ckets by means of huge lugs; the trailer eck was then laboriously raised back to e operating position using the jacks.

Whilst no-one could accuse the roduction Pioneer of appearing modern streamlined in any sense, it did at least ossess a certain brutish charm. This rly machine was a different matter ntirely and, with its upright cab and range 'Mickey Mouse' ears headlamps as clearly a product of another age. The en cab possessed no creature comforts hatsoever, being equipped with little ore than a crude bench seat for the

he first eight production Pioneers, rdered between 1937 and 1939 ontracts V3151, V3270 and V3486), ere fitted with an almost-identical low-ading semi-trailer, albeit rated at 0 tons. This was soon replaced by a ore conventional unit fitted with lding ramps.

crew, and lacking side windows. The narrow, flat windscreen was absolutely perpendicular and the straight-sided cab lacked any curves except for the curious overhanging roof. The proportions of the cab gave the whole thing a rather architectural appearance, resembling a small beach hut on wheels or a Victorian bathing machine. It would be fair to say that it was somewhat ungainly.

It was operated by the Royal Army Ordnance Corps (RAOC) and soon after its delivery the vehicle took part in what were described as 'Tank Brigade exercises'. When these were over, it was turned over to the Royal Army Service Corps (RASC) to allow the 'general design of the vehicle to be assessed'. A few points emerged during the trials and, specifically, the design of the towing pintle was criticised as being easily damaged, and there was adverse comment regarding the difficulties experienced in using the screw jacks with the weight of the tank on them, and the brakes apparently suffered all-too frequent failure. Drivers also complained that the trailer had a tendency to cut in on turns but, of course, this is normal with an articulated vehicle. However, on completion of the trials the machine was stated to have given 'generally satisfactory service mainly due to the simplicity of the design... its chief drawback from a military aspect is its bulk and conspicuousness'.

For five years it remained Britain's only tank transporter, so it is hardly surprising that it was never used for its intended purpose, remaining something of a novelty - after all, it is difficult to move a tank brigade to war if the tanks have to be moved one at a time. Although it ended its days as a training aid, its ultimate fate is not known.

It was to be 1937 before the War Office woke up to the fact that not only were motorised transporters the only practical means of moving tanks from factory to depot, and from depot to war, but that they were going to need lots of them! As one of the official War Office historians said after the War was over 'the history of provision of this type of vehicle follows the depressing path with which readers (of this work) will be becoming familiar'. So, finally, in 1937 the War Office placed the first of many orders with Scammell for an updated version of T22509, complete with removable rear bogie. Pretty soon this evolved into the 20-ton TRMU20 tractor and TRCU20 semi-trailer and then into the production 30-ton Pioneer TRMU20/TRCU30 tank transporter with its ramp-loaded semi-trailer.

But that, as they say, is another story!

THE SCAMMELL MOUNTAINEER

We take a look at an unusual soft-skin personnel carrier

Despite having gone the way of all British heavy-truck manufacturers, Scammell remains a favourite of most military-vehicle enthusiasts. And whilst almost everyone will be familiar with Scammell's WW2 and post-war military models - the Pioneer, Explorer, Constructor and Commander, less well known perhaps is the Mountaineer.

Introduced in 1949, a year before the British Army's Explorer, the Mountaineer was Scammell's first new standard post-war truck. It was a 4x4 chassis which used some of the mechanical components intended for the Explorer and the undersized Bedford-derived cab which was subsequently used on the 6x6 Constructor. At first it employed a transverse leaf-spring suspension for the front axle like the wartime Pioneer, but towards the end of its life, this was replaced by large, exposed coil springs. However, unlike the 6x4 Pioneer, it was equipped with a driven axle - the same axle as was subsequently used on the 6x6 Explorer. At the rear, the single axle was suspended on conventional semi-elliptical springs. Power was provided by either a Scammell-Meadows 6PC650 petrol engine - again the same power unit as was to be fitted to the Explorer - or, latterly, with a Rolls-Royce C6NFL naturally-aspirated six-cylinder diesel. Alternative power units included the Meadows engine in its original 6DC650 diesel format and the Gardner 6LW; after Scammell's takeover by Leyland in 1955, a Leyland diesel was also added to the line-up. Drive was

carried to both axles through a six-speed Scammell gearbox via a single-speed transposing box (as Scammell always described it) to double-reduction axles at front and rear.

With its excellent ground clearance and rugged construction, the Mountaineer was ideal for the developing world where roads were perhaps less reliable and maintenance facilities less available. The chassis was available in a choice of wheelbase lengths and could be fitted with a cargo, dump truck, tanker or other body on a rigid chassis, or equipped with a fifth wheel for use as a tractor; in its later life the vehicle was also available as a wrecker and a number were supplied to Abu Dhabi using Reynold Boughton recovery equipment. Although it was not generally seen as a military vehicle - Scammell preferred to sell it as a heavy hauler for use in tough, export markets - a 1962 technical brochure, aimed specifically at the military sector, shows the Mountaineer equipped as a 120-seat personnel carrier, mobile workshop, water tanker and cargo truck. And despite the wide choice of equipment and configuration, there was a high degree of commonality of automotive equipment across the range.

The Mountaineer is one of Scammell's 'forgotten' models, and the 120-seat articulated personnel carrier, particularly, has rarely appeared in print and almost certainly deserves closer inspection. However, whilst it might sound very grand, this so-called personnel carrier was

really little more than a Rollalong-designed lightweight bus body coupled via a fifth wheel to a Mountaineer prime mover. Very much in the colonial tradition, it was aimed squarely at the Middle Eastern market, though whether it found any success or not is difficult to ascertain.

Technical specification

Nomenclature: tractor, 6-ton, 4x4, equipped as personnel carrier, 120 seat; Scammell Mountaineer.

Engine: Rolls-Royce C6NFL; six-cylinders; 12,176cc; diesel; overhead valves; power output 150bhp at 2100rpm.
Transmission: 6F1R; part-time 4x4.
Suspension: swing axle at front on coil springs (early examples had transverse semi-elliptical spring); live axle at rear on semi-elliptical springs.
Brakes: air pressure.
Construction: steel ladder chassis; steel-panelled cab; semi-trailer uses steel ladder chassis with steel-framed, twin-skin aluminium panelled body.
Electrical system: 24V.

Dimensions
Length (overall), 768in approx; width, 114in; height, 132in. Wheelbase, 204in.

The motive power unit was a 17-foot wheelbase Mountaineer 4x4 powered by a Rolls-Royce C6NFL diesel. Large twin oil-bath air cleaners were fitted presumably to suit the dusty conditions under which it was expected to operate. The part-time driven front axle was suspended on forward-located and very exposed coil springs. A standard SAE/SMMT fifth-wheel unit was bolted across the chassis, and a winch could be provided if required.

The cab was that curiously-undersized two-man unit derived from Bedford pressings and much beloved of Scammell during the 'fifties and sixties. Although it was probably a huge improvement in terms of creature comforts on the traditional coach-built cabs fitted to, for example, the Pioneer and Explorer, it always looked rather mean perched on Scammell's massive trucks, and the typical twin-skin roof always manages to resemble a flat cap. Early Mountaineers had the cycle-type wings of the Pioneer, turning with the wheels, but by the time this machine was introduced in the early 'sixties, these had given way to the huge boxy wings like those fitted to the Leyland Martian.

The trailer body was constructed by Sparshatts on a Cranes drop-frame twin-axle semi-trailer chassis. It was a huge thing, almost 50 feet long and more than nine feet wide and was way outside the statutory limits for European roads. In typical bus-body style, the construction consisted of an inner and outer skin of aluminium panels on a steel frame, and in order to reduce heat gain, glass-fibre insulation was incorporated between the

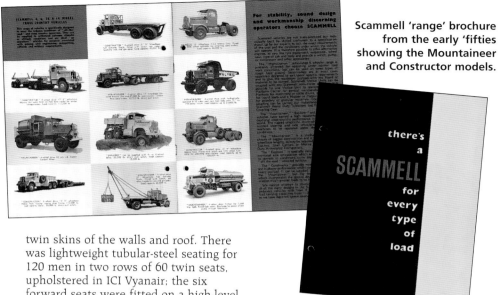

Scammell 'range' brochure from the early 'fifties showing the Mountaineer and Constructor models.

twin skins of the walls and roof. There was lightweight tubular-steel seating for 120 men in two rows of 60 twin seats, upholstered in ICI Vyanair; the six forward seats were fitted on a high-level area above the fifth wheel. Nine half-drop (and removable) windows were fitted along each side and there were fixed windows at the front and rear. Access was provided from the rear via a single hinged door; there was also a side-mounted emergency door.

In deference to its intended area of use, electric air-conditioning equipment was fitted in the front roof dome, and a 40-gallon tank was installed with piping connecting it to a drinking fountain alongside the emergency door.

Although it was a decidedly 'unmilitary-looking' machine, at least three were constructed - does anyone know if any have survived?

Right: Front view of the Mountaineer tractor. Note the exposed coil springs for the swing axle at the front; these had replaced the earlier semi-elliptical leaf spring.

Below and bottom right: Interior views of the body looking towards the front and rear. Note the raised seating platform over the fifth-wheel coupling.

Foreign Explorers

An unusual Scammell Explorer/Constructor hybrid supplied to New Zealand and Egypt

In 1950, the FV11301 Scammell Explorer was introduced into the British Army as a replacement for the WW2 Pioneer. Although it was provided with six-wheel drive, and in a strange break with its predecessor, a hugely thirsty Scammell-Meadows petrol engine, it was very much in the same mould... nevertheless, with a power-to-weight ratio of 13.9bhp/ton, it was a powerful and useful vehicle. But the theme of the times was 'export or die' and unfortunately the antique perpendicular cab and fixed-position sliding jib probably didn't compare well with the more-sophisticated American wreckers and it was to be half a decade before Watford sold any of these babies elsewhere.

IN 1956, the New Zealand government purchased a batch of three, or perhaps four, Explorers for use as medium/heavy recovery vehicles, and in 1959 a number of similar vehicles were sold to the Egyptian government. Scammell's general-

One of the vehicles remains in the New Zealand Army Museum collection.

Technical specification

Nomenclature: truck, 10 ton, medium/heavy recovery, 6x6; Scammell RV 6x6 RR.

Engine: Rolls-Royce C6NFL Series 142A; six cylinders; 12,170cc; diesel; overhead valves; power output 175bhp at 2100rpm; torque 490 lbf/ft at 1275rpm.
Transmission: 6F1Rx2; part-time 6x6.
Suspension: rocking front axle, suspended on transverse semi-elliptical spring; walking beam gearcases at rear, suspended on semi-elliptical springs.
Brakes: air pressure.
Construction: steel ladder chassis; steel cab; steel-framed timber rear body.
Electrical system: 24V.

Dimensions
Length, 248in; width, 105in; height, 116in (to top of cab). Wheelbase, 138in; bogie centres, 51in.
Weight, 26,208 lb.

arrangement drawing, dated March 1956, shows that although the chassis, rear body and recovery equipment were little changed from the British Army version, the vehicle was brought a little more up to date in other areas.

For New Zealand, the Meadows petrol engine was replaced by a Rolls-Royce C6NFL normally-aspirated 12-litre diesel - identical to the engine fitted to the Constructors which the British Army had been buying as prime movers for engineering plant. Egypt, presumably being blessed with cheap petrol, elected to retain the petrol engine used on the British Explorers. Also rejected by both nations

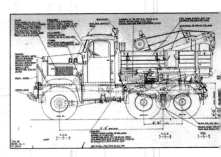

Scammell's general arrangement drawing for the New Zealand Explorer, dated March 1956.

were the antediluvian cab and moving front wings. Again the Constructor came the rescue, providing the more modern a steel two-man enclosed cab which Scammell had developed from Bedford pressings, with the simple cycle-type mudguards replaced by boxy, fixed units. The cab roof retained the distinctive double-skinned 'cap' seen on the British Constructors, and an anti-aircraft ring wa provided above the passenger seat.

Other aspects of the design were unchanged. Scammell's innovative walki beam gearcases were retained at the rear, suspended on semi-elliptical springs, and the front, there was a rocking axle on a single transverse laminated spring, locate by triangulated radius arms on a ball-mount. Like the British version, the recovery equipment consisted of a powe operated 4½-ton extensible jib and a 15-to Scammell vertical winch. Stowage compartments were provided beneath th passenger door for tracks, and at the rear either side of the spare wheel, for person kit.

The combination of the no-nonsense rear body and the stylish cab made for a attractive vehicle and at least two surviv in New Zealand - one is in the Army Museum collection, the other remains in use by a house mover and I'm grateful to Dave Hardway for the photographs.

Scammell Explorer chassis showing the general layout and extreme axle articulation.